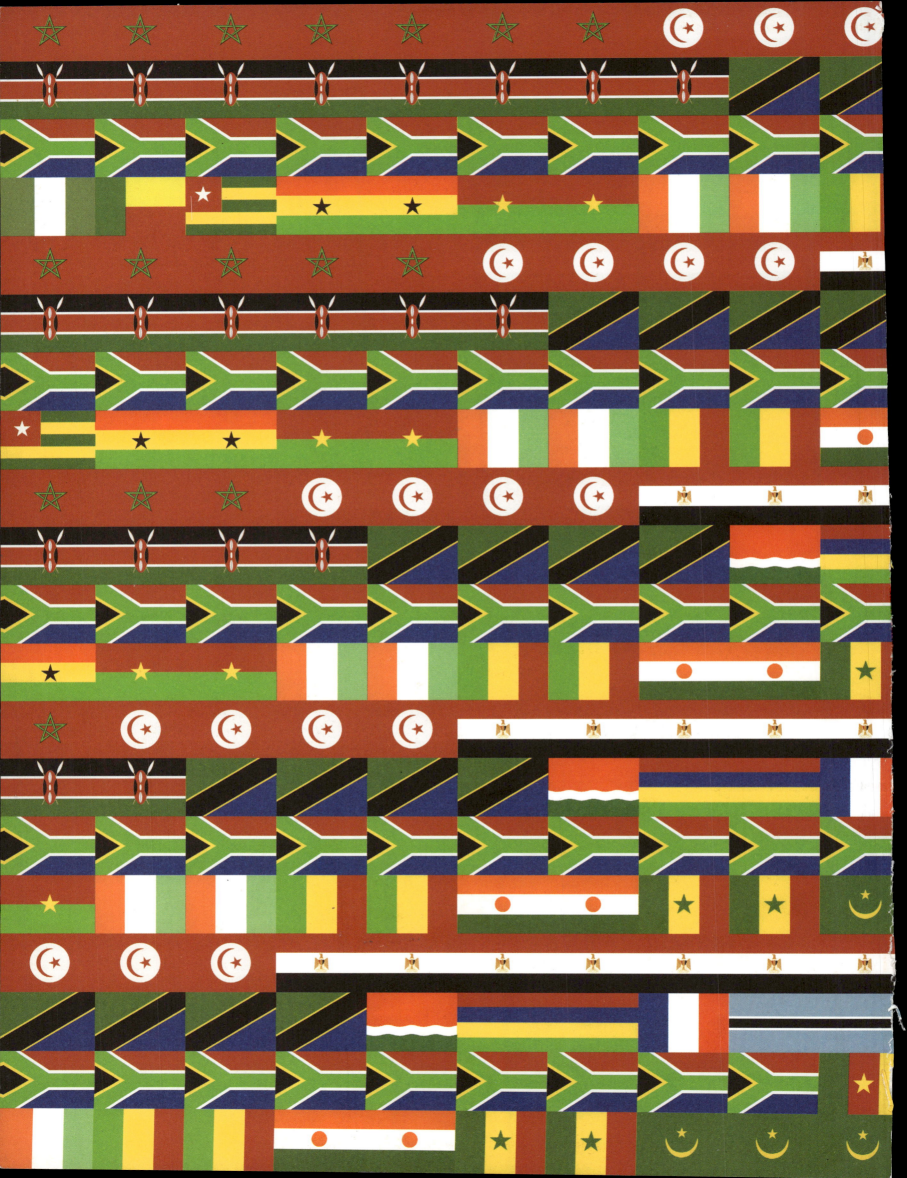

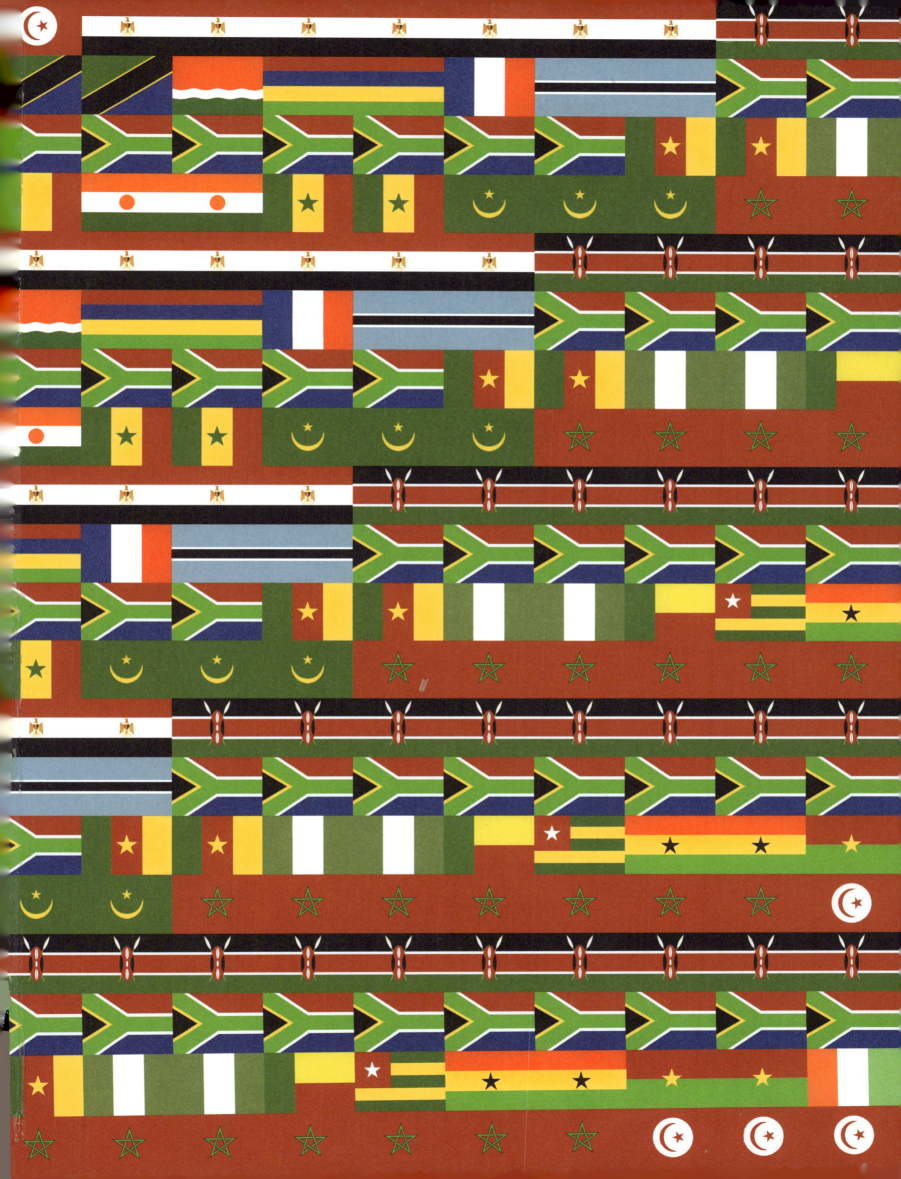

INSIDE AFRICA
NORTH & EAST

PHOTOS BY DEIDI VON SCHAEWEN
TEXT BY FREDERIC COUDERC & LAURENCE DOUGIER
EDITED BY ANGELIKA TASCHEN

INSIDE
AFRICA
NORTH & EAST

TASCHEN

KÖLN LONDON LOS ANGELES MADRID PARIS TOKYO

INTERVIEW WITH DEIDI VON SCHAEWEN

by Michèle Champenois, Paris

After four years of travelling across the continent of Africa, four years of discoveries and encounters from north to south and east to west, what is the African landscape or memory that most immediately springs to your mind?

Oddly enough, I think of the very last evening I spent there, in Agadez, Niger. There was a full moon; the night was magical, seeming to sum up all the marvels and surprises of my many trips to the continent. The job was done; I had visited no fewer than 20 countries, to complete a book which had far outstripped our early expectations. There was a party in progress, in the house of the Swiss artist Not Vital. The walls of the broad courtyard were crowned with cattle horns, standing out against the night sky. Our Tuareg friends were busy preparing a heavily-spiced dish to be served on fresh bread straight from an oven dug in the sand, a real desert oven. As they cooked, they sang to the beat of improvised drums.

Whether you're talking about modern houses or traditional methods of construction, the book seems to have two distinct and alternating lines of approach. Each in its way expresses a quest for harmony, for a way to demonstrate hospitality. The memory you have just mentioned expresses that.

Yes, the moment in Agadez was a unique and rare one. Like so many other people I met in the course of my travels, the people there showed apparently inexhaustible reserves of generosity and kindness. In Africa, peoples' houses resemble them: the ones photographed for the book all spring from the traditions and the natural richness of Africa's landscapes, though so many are threatened. In Agadez, looking back, I felt a sudden spurt of admiration for the countless ingenious ways there are of building, which have allowed African men and women to live in such widely different climates and under so many different conditions.

The book would never have come into existence were it not for my passionate desire to travel, to see, and to understand ever more about this source of harmony. The unexpected and impromptu things that happen to you indicate good fortune; they are the traveller's most cherished companions, and I've had my full share of them.

You've travelled in India. On five continents, you've assembled the most extraordinary examples of art brut and landscapes imagined and laid out by builders, many of whom lay no claim to the status of artist. How does Africa fit into this pattern?

This book has been a crazy enterprise – but it's also a link in the chain. I had just finished Indian Interiors for Taschen, a book on a civilization and a group of peoples that I know well. In Africa I was able to use that book time and again to show exactly what I was up to with this next project. South Africa, where I had already spent a lot of time preparing my book Fantasy Worlds (also published by Taschen), served as my point of departure. By the time I was finished, four and a half years later, I had made over 50 trips by air, in small private planes, helicopters and once even in a military aircraft. I also travelled in buses, boats, on foot, by bush taxi, and on motorbikes. Above all, I rode on the wings of friendship; and I will always be grateful for the way in which friends, old and new, have contributed to the success of my collection of reportages.

Where did you start?

I decided in 1999 to begin the adventure in Cape Town and Johannesburg. In South Africa I knew I could find magnificent modern architecture, observe the life of the townships, and visit the painted houses of the Ndebele, who continue to draw their geometrical frescoes in different shapes and brighter colours than ever before. The whole span of the book was right there in SA – brand new ultra-modern buildings, the painted earth homes of the Ndebele, and the hard struggle in the townships to salvage and use every particle of discarded building material.

Where does contemporary architecture stand in all of this?

There are plenty of fine contemporary buildings throughout Africa; in Morocco you'll see magnificent contemporary interiors, in Mauritius too; also in the hotel sector, in South Africa, in the Ivory Coast and even in Ghana. The more modern and handsome it is, the more it seems to me that recent African architecture looks to be inspired by the age-old rules – whose aim, of course, is secret harmony.

Which was the longest and most complex stage of your journey?

The core of my work awaited me in the heartland of West Africa. In Paris I had obtained nine visas for nine different countries, itself something of a feat; thereafter I flew out to Abidjan to join my friend Pauline, who had been living in Africa for many years. She helped me move through Burkina Faso, Ghana and Togo, visiting the territories of the Lobi, the Kassena and the Tamberma peoples. I learned to sleep on the roofs of houses and to wash with the minimum of water. At night I went to neighbourhood parties and met the women who, at the close of the rainy season, were busy redecorating and painting their homes, contributing in their own way to the fight against ubiquitous concrete building materials. Sometimes I was allowed to enter rooms specially reserved for religious ceremonies, where I was asked not to take any pictures: this side of my travels, unphotographed, was one more way of gaining a more intimate knowledge of these communities. For two months after this, I continued alone through Ghana, Benin, Nigeria, Cameroon and Mali.

You prepare your journeys with infinitely careful research, working with large numbers of contacts. To what extent did you leave room for improvisation, always such a vital ingredient ?

It would take another whole book to describe the frequently chaotic nature of my travels, and the unexpected opportunities that constantly presented themselves to my greedy eyes and ears. For example, at one point I found myself at an astonishing funeral in a village in Ghana, because in a neighbouring town I had happened to notice a carpenter making a coffin in the shape of an elephant. Another time, to get an audience with the king of Abomey, in Benin, I needed the formal introduction of an archaeologist friend in Paris to an orthodox priest, who happened to be a member of the ruling family. The king himself finally received me surrounded by his wives and courtiers, graciously accepting the royal gifts of fruit and live fowls that I brought him.

Were there any other landmark encounters?

Tons. In Nigeria, I at last met with Susanne

Wenger, an Austrian by birth who became a priestess among the Yoruba and has dedicated the last fifty years of her life to the preservation of a sacred grove by the expedient of building temples and altars among the trees. I entered the Yoruba country under full diplomatic and musical protection, in the company of a touring percussion band whose members I had met at the French Cultural Centre in Lome (Togo).

New Year's Day of 2001 found me all alone on a beach in Cameroon, with no festivities whatever in the offing; though before long, travelling in the new millenium, I was invited in Mali by Aminata Traore, an old friend who had become her country's minister of culture. There I sailed down the Niger from Mopti to Timbuktu, with a troop of artists and musicians who had come from other countries to celebrate the culture of Black Africa.

Your predominant theme is the African habitat and the architecture of places where people live. The forms and materials of Africa are used in accordance with widely different codes; they're adapted to their land-scapes and molded by tradition. But still uniformity is a growing threat, specifically the uniformity of industrial building products…

Of course all these ways of life are threatened with extinction. Yet a single example will serve to show how modern materials – and even corrugated iron, which is used abundantly throughout the world because it is so practical and cheap – can yield highly interesting shapes and lines. Consider the multiple conical roofs of the chiefs' compounds in the west of Cameroon. The number of roofs expresses the power of the chief; they sparkle and glitter in the landscape, but because they're kept perfectly proportioned, they manage also to reproduce the ancestral outlines governing such constructions. When I crossed Mauritania, I was intrigued by the many and various clever uses made of scrap metal: an example being the tin cabin, as used for shops and storage facilities by the semi-nomadic people who build them. These constructions are of infinite variety, yet they are all basically the by-product of salvaged diesel and oil barrels.

The value of these strange constructions is the value of creativity in its most immediate form, expressed by the use of salvaged materials. But the greatest sculptural works, the greatest African traditions, seem to be expressed within the landscape by the use of earth and clay as basic materials.

Indeed. I found myself increasingly fascinated by the purity of earth architecture, and by its perfect adaptation to the environment. Throughout the length and breadth of Africa, I was to observe these qualities time and again, in all their endlessly-renewable formal diversity. In Tunisia there are the cave dwellings in the south and the fortified granaries, or ghorfas, on the edge of the Sahara desert. In Cameroon I paid a visit to the northern region and its *obu cases*. These are made of earth, with reinforced walls that make it possible to clamber right up to their tops to carry out repairs. They are a majestic addition to a landscape that is already breathtaking enough.

In the territory of the Dogon in Mali, I remember the ridge road along which every village was a poignant memorial to a great architectural tradition. There we had three punctures in a single day, and all of them were fixed with makeshift tools by men who materialized out of nowhere – another proof of Africa's unfailing zest for improvisation. Other things awaited me, farther up the mountain; a meeting with a spiritual master, and the sight of a great palaver house with its low ceiling to prevent disputes from degenerating into stand-up violence. In this construction everyone has his turn to express himself before a decision is made. This was a building I knew, having admired it many years earlier; I was happy to find its venerable painter still alive and there to greet me.

Then it was the director of another French institute – this time in Kano, Nigeria – who tactfully guided me into the presence of the local emir and made it possible for me to photograph his palace, a superb building entirely constructed of clay. Alas, money from Saudi Arabia has been flooding in of late, that has permitted the construction nearby of a brand new concrete meeting-house.

The simplicity of earth construction is really admirable, but one of the customs best represented in Africa today is that of painted decoration.

Among the Kassena tribes of Burkina Faso, the old style of red and brown painted décor is still used, only the colours have changed to black and white, now that tar is available in the country. The Ndebele still have their geometrical motifs, only nowadays they include portrayals of scenes and objects from daily life. In Mauritania, a thousand kilometers from Nouakshott on the Road of Hope which cuts straight across the desert, I saw the painted houses of Oualata, whose doors and windows are framed with lime-washed motifs. But above all it was in the Soniké villages on the Senegal River, that I and my friend Mucky Wachter found the most beautiful mural paintings imaginable.

If I'm not mistaken, men aren't the only odd creatures that inhabit the African continent. I'm told there are extraordinary animals too …

When you think of African wildlife, you think of elephants and lions and such. They're really extraordinary, it's true, and not just in photographs! But my strangest experience was on the shores of Lake Naivasha, where I saw a large colony of hippos moving from one lake to another in the night. Their huge shapes glided past our silent group in the semi-darkness, while we goggled at them through infra-red binoculars. Hippos are frightening creatures, not to be treated lightly. I thought of them again in Zanzibar, when I was lucky enough to find myself swimming offshore alongside a school of forty dolphins; I was as free in my movements among them, as they were in their demonstrations of friendship.

You're a passionate lover of Africa. What kind of future would you hope to see there?

We're drawn to Africa and intrigued by it. At the same time we know it to be fragile in the extreme, and we've seen how gravely the patterns and imperatives of the industrial West can threaten the ways of life and the ways of building sanctioned by centuries of African experience. Many of the African interiors shown in this book may vanish forever in the next few years. I have tried to do my best to show the boundless beauty and diversity of African houses and interiors, in the broader hope that a better understanding of the continent's heritage – and particularly of this heritage – will give its cultures the strength to regenerate.

Interview mit Deidi von Schaewen

Das Gespräch führte Michèle Champenois, Paris

Sie sind vier Jahre lang von Süden nach Norden, von Osten nach Westen quer durch Afrika gereist. Welche Landschaft haben Sie vor Augen, woran erinnern Sie sich spontan bei all den Entdeckungen und Begegnungen?

Eigenartigerweise an den letzten Abend in Agades, Niger. Es war Vollmond. Diese magische Nacht schien alle Entdeckungen, Überraschungen und Wunder meiner 15 Reisen in sich vereinigen zu wollen. Und ich habe 20 Länder des afrikanischen Kontinents bereist, um dieses Buch zu realisieren. Wir feierten bei dem Schweizer Künstler Not Vital. Die mit Stierhörnern geschmückten Mauern des weitläufigen Innenhofs zeichneten sich gegen den Himmel ab. Im Hof bereiteten Tuareg-Freunde ein scharfes Gericht zu. Es wird auf Brot serviert, frisch gebacken in einem in den Sand gegrabenen Ofen, einem richtigen „Wüstenofen". Der Gesang der Tuareg erfüllte die Nacht, begleitet von rhythmischem Getrommel auf improvisierten Instrumenten.

Das Buch spielt mit unterschiedlichen Auffassungen, wenn sowohl moderne Häuser als auch Zeugnisse traditioneller Bauweisen vorgestellt werden. Und jede zeugt auf ihre Weise von Harmonie und auch Gastfreundschaft, so wie die Erinnerung, die Sie gerade beschrieben haben.

Ja, es war ein unvergesslicher Moment. Wie bei so vielen Menschen, die mir auf meinen vielen Reisen in der ganzen Welt begegnet sind, begegnete mir in Afrika eine große Herzlichkeit und Gastfreundschaft. Die für dieses Buch fotografierten Häuser spiegeln das wider: Sie schöpfen ihre Schönheit aus dem natürlichen Reichtum der Landschaften dieses Kontinents und aus den Traditionen, von denen aber viele bedroht sind. Das Buch zeigt die unzähligen, überaus erfinderischen Bauweisen, die den Menschen das Leben in diesen extrem unterschiedlichen Klimaverhältnissen erst möglich machen. Ohne meine große Reiselust, ohne den Wunsch, mehr zu sehen und zu lernen, hätte dieses Projekt nicht verwirklicht werden können. Unvorhergesehene Ereignisse und der Zufall waren aber immer wertvolle Reisebegleiter.

Sie haben intensiv Indien bereist, und Sie haben auf allen fünf Kontinenten außergewöhnliche Beispiele der Art brut dokumentiert. Diese Bau- und Kunstwerke der Fantasie wurden nach den Vorstellungen ihrer Schöpfer von Baumeistern errichtet, die sich keineswegs immer als Künstler verstanden. Welche Rolle spielt Afrika in diesem Zusammenhang?

Auch wenn das Buch „Fantasy Worlds" (ebenso bei Taschen erschienen), auf das Sie hier anspielen, ein verrücktes Unterfangen war, ist es dennoch ein Glied in einer Kette. Ich hatte bei Taschen bereits den Band „Indien Interieurs" veröffentlicht, ein Buch über Kultur und Bevölkerung eines Landes, das ich sehr gut kenne und das mir für das Afrika-Projekt viele Türen geöffnet hat. Während der Arbeit an „Fantasy Worlds" hatte ich bereits einige Zeit in Südafrika verbracht, deshalb wählte ich dieses Land auch als Ausgangspunkt für dieses Buchprojekt. In den über viereinhalb Jahren meiner Reisen bin ich etwa 50 Mal geflogen, auch mit kleinen Maschinen, Helikoptern, sogar in einem Militärflugzeug. Ich habe aber auch Busse und Schiffe benutzt, musste zu Fuß gehen, mich mit Buschtaxis oder Mopeds fortbewegen … Doch mehr als alle Transportmittel hat mich die Freundschaft weitergebracht … die Freunde, alte oder neue, haben unendlich zum Erfolg dieser Reportagen beigetragen.

Wo hat alles begonnen?

Anfang 1999 habe ich mich unter anderem von Kapstadt und Johannesburg aus auf dieses Abenteuer eingelassen. In Südafrika gibt es nicht nur eine großartige moderne Architektur, ich konnte auch das Leben in den Townships und die bemalten Häuser der Ndebele erkunden. Die Künstler dieses Volkes erneuern ständig die überlieferten geometrischen Wandmalereien mit neuen Mustern und lebhafteren, haltbareren Farben. In Südafrika eröffnete sich mir die ganze Bandbreite des Buches: vom hoch modernen Haus über die bemalten Lehmhäuser der Ndebele bis zur „Recyclemanie" in den Townships.

Welche Rolle spielt bei all dem die zeitgenössische Architektur?

Schöne Beispiele finden sich im Norden ebenso wie im Süden: in Marokko, wo die Interieurs sehr modern sind, auch in verschiedenen Hotelbauten auf der Insel Mauritius, in Südafrika, an der Elfenbeinküste und sogar in Ghana.

Je moderner und gelungener die zeitgenössischen Interieurs sind, umso mehr orientieren sie sich an alten Regeln und Traditionen, vielleicht auf der Suche nach einer verborgenen Harmonie.

Welches war der längste und komplexeste Abschnitt der Reise?

Der wichtigste Teil meiner Arbeit wartete im Zentrum Westafrikas. Es war mir gelungen, in Paris Visa für neun Länder zu ergattern, was an sich schon eine ganze Reise war. Anschließend traf ich mich in Abidjan mit meiner Freundin Pauline, die selbst in Afrika lebt. Sie half mir auf der Reise durch Burkina Faso, Ghana und Togo in den Gebieten der Lobi, Kassena und Tamberma, wo wir auf Dächern schliefen und lernten, uns mit möglichst wenig Wasser zu waschen. Wir nahmen an nächtlichen Festen teil, trafen Frauen, die nach der Regenzeit ihre Häuser neu schmücken und bemalen und so auf ihre Weise gegen das Vordringen der Betonbauweise kämpfen. Man gab mir hier und da die Erlaubnis, Räume zu betreten, die sonst nur Zeremonien vorbehalten sind, in denen ich allerdings nicht fotografieren durfte. Dieser undokumentierte Teil meiner Reise verhalf mir zu einem tieferen Verständnis für die Einwohner dieser Gegend. Dann bereiste ich in den darauf folgenden beiden Monaten alleine die Länder Ghana, Benin, Nigeria, Kamerun und Mali.

Sie bereiten Ihre Reisen durch ausgiebige Recherche und zahlreiche Kontakte sehr gründlich vor. Welche Bedeutung hat da noch die Improvisation, die unersetzliche Freiheit des Reisenden?

Es ist nicht möglich, in wenigen Worten die zeitweise chaotischen Reisebedingungen zu beschreiben. Doch dem aufmerksamen Beobachter bieten sich immer wieder Gelegenheiten, Unerwartetes zu entdecken. Wie etwa das feierliche Begräbnis in Ghana, an dem ich teilnehmen konnte, weil ich zufällig bei einem Schreiner der Nachbarstadt einen Sarg in Form eines Elefanten entdeckt hatte. Für die Begegnung mit dem König von Abomey in Benin hingegen bedurfte es der formellen Einführung durch einen befreundeten Pariser Archäologen bei einem orthodoxen Priester, der zur königlichen Familie gehörte. Der Herrscher empfing uns im Kreise seiner Frauen und Höflinge und akzeptierte gnädig unser Geschenk, arrangiert aus Früchten und piepsendem Geflügel.

Gab es weitere herausragende Begegnungen?

Ja, sicher. In Nigeria traf ich endlich die gebürtige Österreicherin Susanne Wenger, was schon seit langem mein Wunsch war. Sie wurde dort Priesterin der

Yoruba und widmet sich seit 50 Jahren der Rettung des heiligen Hains, indem sie dort Tempel und Altäre baut. Ich war im Schutz von Diplomatie und Musik nach Nigeria eingereist, zusammen mit einem Orchester tourender Percussionisten, die ich im französischen Kulturzentrum von Lomé in Togo getroffen hatte.

Dann begrüßte ich das Jahr 2001, fern aller Festivitäten, alleine an einem Strand in Kamerun. Unterwegs im neuen Jahrtausend wurde ich in Mali von meiner langjährigen Freundin Aminata Traoré, der ehemaligen Ministerin für Kultur, eingeladen, mit einem Schiff den Niger von Mopti nach Timbuktu hinunterzufahren, und zwar in Begleitung von Künstlern und Musikern aus verschiedenen Ländern, die ihre schwarzafrikanische Kultur feierten.

Ihr Hauptthema ist das Wohnen, die Architektur von Lebensräumen. In Afrika folgt der Umgang mit Formen und Materialien unterschiedlichen Gesetzmäßigkeiten, er passt sich der Umgebung an und ist durch Traditionen geprägt. Und doch lässt sich eine Uniformität nicht aufhalten, insbesondere durch den Rückgriff auf industrielle Produkte.

All diese Lebensformen drohen in der Tat zu verschwinden. Jedoch auch neuere Materialien, ja sogar Blech, das auf allen fünf Kontinenten sehr oft verwendet wird, weil es praktisch und preisgünstig ist, kann zu interessanten Formen inspirieren. Ich habe es im Westen Kameruns gesehen, als ich die vielen konischen Dächer der Chefferien (die Macht des Chefs ist an der Zahl der Dächer abzulesen) fotografiert habe. Das glänzende Wellblech leuchtet in der Landschaft, es ist gut proportioniert und wahrt die traditionelle Form dieser Bauwerke. Ein anderer Gebrauch von Metall hat mich auf der Durchreise durch Mauretanien sehr beeindruckt: Die Blechhütten, die die halbnomadischen Völker in praller Sonne errichtet haben und die entweder als Läden oder als Vorratshütten dienen. Diese Ansammlungen von wieder verwertbarem Material sind äußerst erfindungsreich, abhängig von den zufälligen Funden der Diesel- oder Benzinkanister.

Die Bedeutung dieser ungewöhnlichen Konstruktionen liegt ohne Zweifel in der spontanen Kreativität bei der Verwendung von Recyclingmaterial. Aber nehmen die großen skulpturalen Werke, die großen Traditionen nicht eher in Form von Lehm und Ton Gestalt an?

Ja, das ist wahr. Besonders fasziniert mich immer wieder die Architektur aus Lehm, die sich auf so bemerkenswerte Weise an ihre Umgebung anpasst. Ihre perfekten Proportionen, ihre eleganten, klaren Linien findet man in vielerlei Variationen auf dem gesamten Kontinent. Im Süden Tunesiens sind es die Höhlenwohnungen und die *ghorfas* (befestigte Speicher) am Rande der Sahara. Im Norden Kameruns besuchte ich die Gegend der *obu*-Hütten. Sie sind aus Lehm gebaut, die Wände durch Rippen verstärkt, damit man bei nötigen Reparaturen bis zur Spitze hochsteigen kann. Sie fügen sich auf majestätische Weise in die an sich bereits erstaunliche Landschaft.

Ich erinnere mich an einen Weg auf dem Bergkamm in Mali, im Land der Dogon, wo jedes Dorf wie ein lebendes Monument wirkt, wie ein eindringliches architektonisches Zeugnis. Nur am Rande erwähnt: Damals gaben an einem einzigen Tag drei Autoreifen den Geist auf. Und jedes Mal wurden sie sofort und fast ohne Werkzeug von Männern repariert, die aus dem Nichts aufgetaucht waren – ein weiterer Beweis für die unerschöpfliche Kreativität der Menschen dieses Kontinents. Andere bewegende Ereignisse standen mir noch bevor. So die Begegnung mit einem Hohepriester hoch oben auf den Klippen und der erneute Besuch einer Palaverstätte mit ihrem Versammlungsraum, dessen niedrig angelegte Decke jeden Streit im Keim ersticken soll und wo Entscheidungen erst dann gefällt werden, wenn alle Anwesenden einmal zu Wort gekommen sind. Ich hatte diesen Ort bereits vor Jahren bewundert und freute mich sehr, auch den alten Maler dort wiederzutreffen, dessen Werke die Außenwände schmücken.

Der tatkräftigen Unterstützung des Direktors einer anderen französischen Institution in Kano im Norden Nigerias habe ich es zu verdanken, dass ich bereits nach einer knappen Woche Kontakt zum ortsansässigen Emir herstellen konnte. Dieser erlaubte mir, seinen Palast zu fotografieren, ein einmalig schönes Bauwerk aus Lehm, ebenso eindrucksvoll wie bedroht. Mit saudiarabischen Fonds wurde schon in unmittelbarer Nähe ein Versammlungssaal gebaut ... aus Beton.

Die Schlichtheit der Lehmbauten ist zweifelsohne bewundernswert, doch einer der verbreitetsten Bräuche in Afrika ist die farbige Wandbemalung.

Bei den Stämmen der Kassena in Burkina Faso wurden die Wände ursprünglich rot-braun bemalt.

Diese Tradition wird seit der Einführung von Teer mit schwarzen Mustern auf weißen Wänden fortgesetzt. Bei den Ndebele findet man bunte geometrische Motive wie eh und je, in die sie heute jedoch alltägliche Szenen und Objekte integrieren. In Mauretanien fuhr ich, 1000 Kilometer von Nouakchott entfernt, auf der „Straße der Hoffnung" durch bis nach Oualata, um die berühmten bemalten Häuser zu sehen, deren Türen und Fenster von Ornamenten aus einer Mischung aus Sand und Kalk eingerahmt sind. Doch die schönsten Wandmalereien, die ich je gesehen habe, entdeckte ich mit meiner Freundin Mucky Wachter in den Dörfern der Soninke im Gebiet des Flusses Senegal.

Soweit ich weiß, leben auf dem afrikanischen Kontinent nicht nur Menschen. Man sagt, dass auch die Tiere außergewöhnlich sind ...

Bei den Tieren Afrikas denkt man sofort an Elefanten, Löwen, Nashörner. Sie sind wirklich außergewöhnlich und in der Natur viel beeindruckender als auf einem Foto. Mein unvergesslichstes Erlebnis aber hatte ich am Ufer des Sees Naivasha in Kenia, wo eine große Population von Flusspferden jeden Tag von einem See zum anderen wandert. Bei Einbruch der Dunkelheit zogen diese Tiere mit ihren unheimlichen Körpermassen an unserer kleinen Gruppe vorbei. Wir verhielten uns absolut ruhig, ausgestattet mit Nachtsichtgeräten, denn Flusspferde gehören zu den gefährlichsten Tieren überhaupt. An dieses Erlebnis musste ich auch denken, als ich auf hoher See vor Sansibar das unglaubliche Glück hatte, frei und unbeschwert in einer Gruppe von 40 freundlich gesonnenen Delfinen zu schwimmen.

Sie haben eine große Leidenschaft für Afrika. Was wünschen Sie diesem Kontinent?

Afrika ist ohne Zweifel gleichermaßen anziehend wie beunruhigend, unter anderem, weil es so verletzlich ist. Wir wissen nur zu gut, dass die Modelle des industriellen Westens, mit den aus ihnen resultierenden Zwängen, die über Jahrhunderte erprobten Lebens- und Bauweisen Afrikas bedrohen. Viele der in diesen beiden Bänden enthüllten Intérieurs könnten im Laufe der nächsten Jahre verschwinden. Ich wollte in dieser Publikation die umwerfende Schönheit des schwarzen Kontinents in all seiner Vielfalt zeigen – nicht zuletzt in der Hoffnung, dass eine bessere Kenntnis dieses Kulturerbes hilft, es zu bewahren.

Entretien avec Deidi von Schaewen

Propos recueillis par Michèle Champenois, Paris

Au terme de ces quatre années de voyages à travers le continent africain, de découvertes et de rencontres, du sud au nord et d'est en ouest, quel paysage, quel souvenir vous vient immédiatement à l'esprit?

Curieusement, c'est le dernier soir passé en Afrique, à Agadez, au Niger. Une nuit de pleine lune, magique comme si elle devait résumer les merveilles et les surprises des 15 reportages entrepris dans 20 pays différents pour réaliser ce livre qui a dépassé les espérances initiales. C'est un soir de fête, chez l'artiste suisse Not Vital. Dans la cour immense dont les hauts murs surmontés de cornes de bovins se découpent sur le ciel sombre, ses amis touareg préparent un plat très épicé qui sera servi sur les pains sortis d'un four creusé à même le sable, véritable fourneau du désert. Des rythmes frappés sur des instruments improvisés accompagnent un chant qui monte dans la nuit.

Maisons modernes ou témoignages de traditions constructives, votre ouvrage fait alterner deux approches. On devine qu'elles répondent, de manière différente, à une recherche d'harmonie, à une manière d'exprimer l'hospitalité, comme le souvenir que vous évoquez.

Oui, c'est un moment singulier, à l'image des rencontres faites au long de ces voyages et des ressources inépuisables de l'hospitalité et de la gentillesse des habitants. Les maisons photographiées pour ce livre puisent leur beauté dans la richesse naturelle des paysages du continent et dans les traditions dont beaucoup sont menacées. Ce livre se veut un hommage aux mille manières de construire, tellement inventives, qui ont permis aux hommes de vivre sous tous les climats. Il n'existerait pas sans la passion que suscite un tel voyage, le désir d'en voir et d'en savoir plus. Solutions imprévues, départs impromptus, la chance est toujours le bagage essentiel du voyageur.

Vous avez parcouru l'Inde, mais aussi rassemblé sur les cinq continents des exemples extraordinaires d'art brut, de paysages construits sous la dictée de leur imaginaire par des bâtisseurs qui n'ont pas toujours le titre d'artistes. Comment se situe l'Afrique sur ce parcours?

Si ce livre est une entreprise un peu folle, il est aussi un maillon. J'avais terminé les «Intérieurs de l'Inde» (publié par Taschen), une civilisation et des peuples que je connais bien, et le livre sur l'Inde a souvent été mon ambassadeur pour expliquer le projet. L'Afrique du Sud, où j'avais déjà passé beaucoup de temps pour préparer «Fantasy Worlds» (Taschen), m'a servi de point de départ. En quatre ans et demi, j'ai pris l'avion une cinquantaine de fois, des petits coucous, des hélicoptères et même un avion militaire, mais je me suis aussi déplacée en bus, en bateau, à pied, en taxi-brousse, en mobylette. Et surtout sur les ailes de l'amitié... Je ne dirai jamais assez à quel point les amis, anciens ou nouveaux, ont contribué à la réussite de ces reportages.

Par où commencer?

J'ai choisi, dès 1999, Cape Town, Johannesburg et l'Afrique du Sud pour engager cette aventure, un pays où je pouvais trouver de magnifiques architectures modernes, autant qu'observer la vie des townships et m'approcher des maisons peintes des Ndebele qui continuent à tracer leurs fresques géométriques en renouvelant les trames et les couleurs, désormais beaucoup plus vives. Déjà, tout le thème du livre était là: de la maison la plus moderne aux maisons de terre peintes des Ndebele, jusqu'à la frénésie de récupération dans les bidonvilles.

Quelle est la place de l'architecture contemporaine?

On en trouve de beaux exemples, du Nord au Sud: au Maroc avec des intérieurs très contemporains, à l'Île Maurice, dans l'hôtellerie, en Afrique du Sud, en Côte-d'Ivoire et même au Ghana. Plus elles sont modernes et réussies, plus les créations récentes s'inspirent de règles anciennes, à la recherche d'une harmonie secrète.

Quel a été votre périple le plus long, le plus complexe?

Il me fallait aborder le vif du sujet, le centre de l'Afrique occidentale. Ayant décroché neuf visas pour neuf pays à Paris, une sorte d'épopée en soi, j'ai rejoint à Abidjan Pauline, une amie installée en Afrique et qui allait m'aider à parcourir, au Burkina Faso, au Ghana et au Togo, les territoires des Lobis, des Kassenas et des Tambermas. Cela signifiait dormir sur le toit des maisons, apprendre à se laver avec très peu d'eau, assister à des fêtes nocturnes, rencontrer ces femmes qui, après la saison des pluies, redécorent et peignent leurs maisons et luttent ainsi à leur manière contre l'avancée universelle du parpaing de béton. Être admise, parfois, dans des pièces réservées aux cérémonies où l'on me demandait de ne pas faire de photos. Ce périple, entre deux prises de vues, était aussi une manière d'avancer dans la connaissance intime de ces communautés. Pendant deux mois, j'ai continué, seule, vers le Ghana, le Bénin, le Nigeria, le Cameroun, et le Mali.

Vous préparez vos déplacements par un travail intense de documentation et de nombreux contacts. Quelle est la part de l'improvisation, cette irremplaçable liberté du voyageur?

Impossible de détailler en quelques lignes les conditions parfois chaotiques des déplacements. Mais, bien sûr, si on prête l'oreille, les occasions inattendues de découvrir autre chose sont fréquentes. Je me souviens de ces funérailles solennelles, dans un village du Ghana, auxquelles j'ai pu assister parce que, chez le menuisier de la ville voisine, la préparation d'un cercueil en forme d'éléphant m'avait intriguée et que j'avais interrogé l'artisan.

En revanche, pour rencontrer le roi d'Abomey, au Benin, il m'a fallu une introduction officielle, celle qu'un ami archéologue parisien m'avait proposée, auprès d'un prêtre orthodoxe, membre de la famille régnante. Le roi, entouré de ses femmes et de sa cour, nous a reçus et a accepté les fruits et les volailles piaillantes que nous lui apportions.

D'autres rencontres marquantes?

Bien sûr. Au Nigeria, j'ai pu enfin rencontrer Susanne Wenger. Cette Autrichienne, devenue prêtresse chez les Yoruba, consacre sa vie, depuis 50 ans, au sauvetage de la forêt sacrée en y bâtissant des temples et des autels. Une autre fois, c'est en compagnie d'un orchestre de percussionnistes en tournée, rencontrés au centre culturel français de Lomé, au Togo, que je suis entrée dans le pays, sous protection diplomatique... et musicale.

Seule sur une plage du Cameroun, j'ai franchi, loin de toutes festivités, le passage à l'an 2001. En route vers un nouveau millénaire, j'ai aussi été invitée au Mali par Aminata Traoré, une amie de longue date

devenue ministre de la culture de son pays, à descendre le fleuve Niger de Mopti à Tombouctou, avec des artistes et des musiciens venus de plusieurs pays célébrer les cultures de l'Afrique noire.

Votre thème central, c'est l'habitat, l'architecture des lieux de vie. Les formes, les matériaux sont travaillés selon des codes très variés, adaptés aux paysages et forgés par les traditions. Mais l'uniformisation guette, notamment à cause du recours à des produits industriels …

Evidemment, tous ces modes de vie sont menacés… de disparition. Pourtant, même un matériau récent, comme la tôle, utilisée couramment sur les cinq continents parce qu'elle est pratique et peu coûteuse, peut se prêter à des lignes intéressantes. Je l'ai vu, dans l'ouest du Cameroun, où j'ai photographié des chefferies avec leurs toits coniques multiples (la puissance du chef est fonction de leur nombre), auxquels la tôle confère une brillance remarquable dans le paysage mais qui, parce qu'ils restent bien proportionnés, respectent les silhouettes ancestrales de ces constructions.

En traversant la Mauritanie, j'ai été aussi vivement intéressée par l'usage qui y est fait du métal: des cabanes en tôle, dressées en plein soleil, servent soit de boutiques soit d'entrepôts à des populations seminomades. Ces assemblages de récupération sont des plus inventifs, au hasard des trouvailles de barils de gasoil ou de pétrole.

Ce qui fait la valeur de ces étrangetés, c'est sans doute la créativité dans son expression la plus immédiate, à partir des matériaux de récupération. Mais les grandes œuvres sculpturales, les grandes traditions, c'est plutôt en terre qu'elles prennent forme dans le paysage.

Oui, l'architecture en terre me fascine pour sa pureté, son équilibre et son adaptation remarquable à l'environnement. J'ai eu souvent l'occasion, du nord au sud du continent, de vérifier ces qualités, toujours renouvelées dans leur diversité. En Tunisie, ce sont les maisons troglodytes, dans le sud, et les *ghorfas*, ces greniers fortifiés, aux portes du Sahara. Au Cameroun, j'ai arpenté, au nord, la région des cases-obus. Façonnées en terre, dotées de parois renforcées qui permettent d'accéder au sommet pour les réparations,

elles s'imposent en majesté dans un paysage lui-même étonnant.

Au Mali, dans le pays Dogon, je me souviens de ce chemin de crête, où chaque village est un monument vivant, un témoignage poignant d'architecture. Juste pour l'anecdote, trois pneus crevés dans la même journée, ont été réparés sur place sans outillage par des hommes apparus de nulle part, nouvelle preuve d'inventivité sans limite … Mais j'ai aussi connu d'autres émotions dans cette région: la rencontre d'un grand féticheur, sur la falaise; et les retrouvailles avec une maison de palabre, cette grande structure basse de plafond pour décourager toute dispute où l'on discute chaque décision en donnant la parole à chacun. Je l'avais admirée il y a des années. Le vieux peintre que j'avais vu était toujours là lui aussi …

Au nord du Nigeria, avec l'aide du directeur de l'institut français de Kano, j'ai pu entrer en contact, au bout d'une petite semaine, avec l'émir du lieu afin que celui-ci m'autorise à photographier son palais, un superbe édifice en terre, aussi remarquable que menacé. C'est que déjà, hélas, des fonds provenant d'Arabie saoudite ont servi à financer la construction, toute proche, d'une salle de réunion … toute en béton.

La simplicité de la terre est admirable, certainement, mais l'une des coutumes les mieux représentées en Afrique est le décor peint.

Dans les tribus Kassenas, au Burkina Faso, les anciennes peintures rouge et brun se perpétuent, mais en noir et blanc, avec l'arrivée du goudron. Chez les Ndebele, on trouve toujours des motifs à base géométrique dans lesquels ils insèrent aujourd'hui des scènes ou des objets de la vie quotidienne. En Mauritanie, à 1000 kilomètres de Nouakchott, sur la «route de l'Espoir», qui part tout droit à travers le désert, je suis allée sans hésiter jusqu'aux maisons peintes de Oualata, où les portes et les fenêtres sont bordées de motifs à la chaux. Mais c'est surtout dans les villages Soninke, dans la région du fleuve Sénégal, que nous avons trouvé, avec mon amie Mucky Wachter, les peintures murales les plus belles que j'aie jamais vues.

Si j'ai bien compris, les hommes ne sont pas seuls à habiter le continent africain. On dit qu'il y a des animaux extraordinaires …

Quand on pense aux animaux d'Afrique, on songe tout de suite aux éléphants, aux lions, aux rhinocéros. Ils sont extraordinaires, c'est vrai, et beaucoup plus qu'en photo! Quant à moi, j'ai vécu le moment le plus inouï au bord du lac Naivasha, où une importante colonie d'hippopotames se déplace chaque jour d'un plan d'eau à l'autre. À la tombée de la nuit, les bêtes ont frôlé de leur masse inquiétante notre petit groupe d'individus silencieux et armés de jumelles à infrarouges. Pas question d'approcher ces animaux parmi les plus redoutables. J'y ai repensé plus tard, lorsqu'au large de Zanzibar, j'ai eu la chance de nager au milieu d'une quarantaine de dauphins, libre de mes mouvements comme eux de leurs démonstrations d'affection.

On comprend que vous êtes une amie passionnée de l'Afrique. Que lui souhaitez-vous?

Si l'Afrique attire et intrigue à juste titre, c'est aussi parce qu'elle est fragile. Nous savons combien les modèles et les impératifs de l'Occident industriel menacent les modes de vie et les manières de bâtir consacrés par des siècles d'expérience. Beaucoup des intérieurs d'Afrique dévoilés dans cet ouvrage risquent de disparaître dans les prochaines années. Ce livre vise à faire découvrir l'immense beauté du continent noir dans sa diversité. En espérant qu'une meilleure connaissance du patrimoine aidera ces cultures à se perpétuer.

MOROCCO

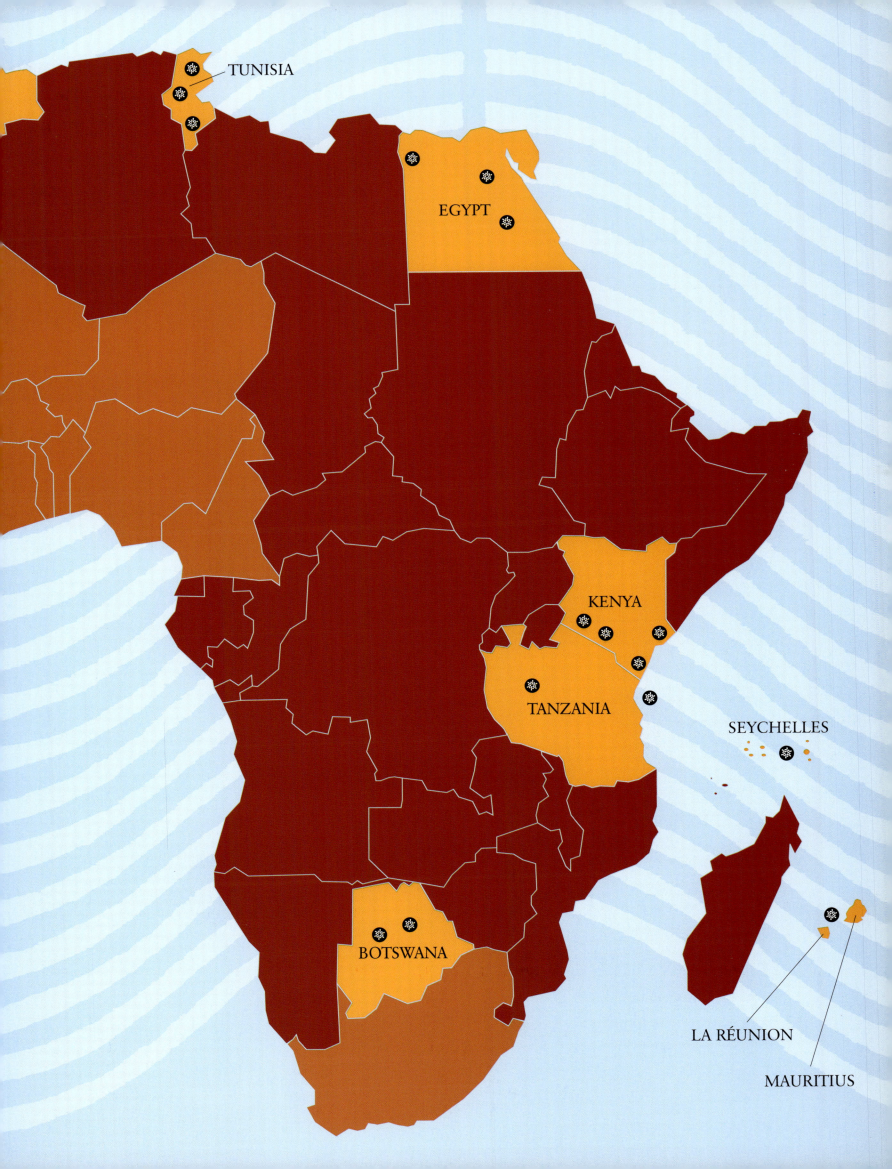

TUNISIA

EGYPT

KENYA

TANZANIA

SEYCHELLES

BOTSWANA

LA RÉUNION

MAURITIUS

Dar Moulay Boubker

Dar Badi

Carla & Franca Sozzani

Dar Karma

Dar El Hanna

Aït Bou Goumez
& Ouarzazate

MOROCCO

CARLA & FRANCA SOZZANI

MARRAKESH

The Casa Sozzani, decorated by an American artist,
offers a new brand of orientalism in the heart of the medina.

A 12th century mosque with Spanish-Moorish minaret marks the entrance to Marrakesh's medina. Here, in the maze of alleys and *souks*, a pair of Italian sisters have made their home. Carla Sozzani is the founder of the Corso Como boutique in Milan, and her sister Franca is a top editor with Condé Nast Italy.

Drawing on the combined experience of their two careers, they have transformed two Marrakesh *riyads*, turning old ruined patios into pools and gardens filled with banana trees. It took three years of dedicated restoration work, with Kris Ruh, an American artist who lives between Marrakesh and Italy, putting together the various elements of the décor. From the door and window frames, whose columns are entwined with metal foliage, to the curtain rods, radiator grilles and wrought iron bed heads, right through to the metal tube chandeliers picked up at the city dump, every element was something for Ruh to use creatively and differently. The spaces are extraordinary, as are the fabrics and the colours. You're about to be overwhelmed completely when someone quietly takes you by the hand. There's mint tea waiting on the terrace, which is one of the highest in the medina. You can see as far as the Atlas mountains from here. "This isn't quite reality," murmurs Franca Sozzani. But *chi lo sa?*

Hinter der Moschee aus dem 12. Jahrhundert beginnt das Labyrinth der Gassen, in dem sich zwei italienische Schwestern niedergelassen haben. Während Carla Sozzani eine Galerie am Corso Como in Mailand betreibt, betreut ihre Schwester Franca im Verlag Condé Nast verschiedene Magazine.

Im Bewusstsein ihrer langjährigen Berufserfahrungen schufen sie innerhalb von drei Jahren aus zwei miteinander verbundenen *riyads* ein neues Anwesen. Intensive Restaurationsarbeiten waren vonnöten; so wurde ein Patio in einen Pool und der andere in einen Garten voller Bananenstauden verwandelt. Kris Ruh, ein amerikanischer Künstler, der zwischen Italien und Marrakesch pendelt, übernahm die Ausstattung. Ziel seiner Kreativität waren ebenso die Tür- und Fensterrahmen wie die verkleideten Heizkörper, Gardinenstangen und das Kopfteil eines Bettes mit schmiedeeisernen Schlangen. Der Künstler verwandelte das Gebäude in all seinen Bestandteilen, sodass sich der Betrachter heute nicht satt sehen kann am allgegenwärtigen Farbenspiel, an der Vielfalt der Einrichtungsgegenstände, der Stoffe und Gewebe. Doch schon bald werden wir weitergeführt, denn auf der Terrasse – einer der höchst gelegenen in der ganzen Stadt – erwartet uns bereits der Pfefferminztee. Von hier aus kann man sogar das Atlasgebirge erkennen. »Zu schön, um wahr zu sein«, bekräftigt Franca Sozzani.

La mosquée du 12ᵉ siècle et son minaret hispano-mauresque signalent l'entrée du labyrinthe. Ici, dans l'écheveau des ruelles et le lacis des souks, deux sœurs italiennes ont établi leur résidence. Carla Sozzani est la fondatrice de la boutique Corso Como à Milan, sa sœur Franca cumule les responsabilités éditoriales chez Condé Nast Italie.

Déroulant le fil des mérites glanés au cours de leur carrière, elles ont transfiguré deux riyads en trois années de restauration. Les patios sont devenus piscine et jardins agrémentés de bananiers. Kris Ruh, artiste américain partagé entre Marrakech et l'Italie, a conçu les éléments du décor. Des encadrements de portes et fenêtres aux colonnes habillées de feuillage en métal, des tringles à rideaux, cache radiateur ou tête de lit à serpent en fer forgé, aux lustres en tubes de métal dénichés à la décharge de la ville, tout élément fut, pour l'artiste, matière à détournement et création. Volumes des pièces, jeu de couleurs, étoffes en pagaille, l'œil ne sait plus où s'attarder. Mais vite, on vous prend par la main. Le thé à la menthe est servi sur la terrasse, l'une des plus élevées de la médina. Le regard porte jusqu'à l'Atlas. «Ce n'est pas la réalité», admet Franca Sozzani. Mais, *Chi lo sa?*

✳ **FACING PAGE** The *riyad* is full of corners where people can meet quietly or just be alone – such as this tiny salon in the corridor, with Indian fabrics and rugs on a floor of cement squares. ✳ **RECHTE SEITE** Der *riyad* verfügt über diverse Ecken, die sich als Treffpunkte oder als Orte des Rückzugs eignen, wie dieser kleine Salon. Auf dem Mosaikboden liegen indische Teppiche. ✳ **PAGE DE DROITE** Le riyad recèle des recoins conçus en lieux de retrouvailles ou de solitude comme ce petit salon de détente aménagé dans le long corridor où tapis et étoffes indiennes recouvrent un sol en carreaux de ciment.

✳ **ABOVE** In the dining room, a sari serves as a tablecloth and a painted tree flickers with candles. **FACING PAGE** The salon on the second floor, with its wrought iron chandelier and, at the centre of the room, a black ottoman. ✳ **OBEN** Ein Sari dient Carla und Franca Sozzani in ihrem Speisezimmer als Tischtuch. Mildes Kerzenlicht beleuchtet das Wandbild eines Baumes. **RECHTS** Der Salon im zweiten Stock mit dem schmiedeeisernen Lüster und der schwarzen Ottomane in der Mitte. ✳ **CI-DESSUS** Dans la salle à manger, un sari tient lieu de nappe. Face aux convives, un arbre peint scintille à la lueur des bougies. **PAGE DE DROITE** Le salon du deuxième étage avec son lustre en fer forgé et l'ottomane noire au milieu de la pièce.

※ **FACING PAGE** A mix of cultures in this small salon: Kris Ruh's creations go well with the traditional motifs of the seat and the ceiling. **ABOVE** Carla Sozzani's daughter Sara has a bedroom facing the banana trees in the patio. Pastel-coloured walls and an old silk counterpane. ※ **LINKE SEITE** Bunter Kulturmix im kleinen Salon: Die Wiederaufnahme traditioneller Muster durch den Künstler wurde hier konsequent durchgeführt. **OBEN** Das Zimmer von Sara, der Tochter Carla Sozzanis, gibt den Blick frei auf die Bananenstauden des Patios. Die Mauer ist pastellfarben, die Tagesdecke aus alter Chinaseide gefertigt. ※ **PAGE DE GAUCHE** Mélange des cultures dans ce petit salon; les créations de Kris Ruh s'accordent aux motifs traditionnels visibles du siège au plafond. **CI-DESSUS** La fille de Carla Sozzani, Sara, dispose d'une chambre face aux bananiers du patio. Mur pastel et dessus-de-lit en soie ancienne.

❋ **ABOVE** Franca's son's bedroom. **FACING PAGE** The bathroom antechamber, with the bath behind the hanging fabrics. Gianfranco Ferré, a frequent visitor, calls the Casa Sozzani "A modern version of a tale from the Thousand and One Nights". ❋ **OBEN** Das Zimmer von Francas Sohn. **RECHTE SEITE** Das Vorzimmer des hinter dem Vorhang gelegenen Bades. Gianfranco Ferré, ein häufiger Gast, schwärmt von der Casa Sozzani: »Eine moderne Version einer Residenz aus Tausendundeiner Nacht.« ❋ **CI-DESSUS** La chambre du fils de Franca. **PAGE DE DROITE** Antichambre de la salle de bains, située derrière les étoffes. Gianfranco Ferré, habitué des lieux, admire la *casa* Sozzani: «C'est la version moderne d'un conte des Mille et Une Nuits.»

✳ **FACING PAGE** The entrance to Franca's bedroom, with carpets. **ABOVE** Star chandeliers from the souks of Marrakesh combine with the yellowed glass of the windows to flood this bathroom in golden light. **FOLLOWING PAGES** Meals are prepared under the starlit kitchen ceiling and served by staff wearing traditional clothes. ✳ **LINKS** Der mit Teppichen verzierte Eingang zu Francas Zimmer. **OBEN** Die Lichter der Souks von Marrakesch fallen durch die gelb getönten Scheiben und tauchen das Bad in goldenen Glanz. **FOLGENDE DOPPELSEITE** Das traditionell gekleidete Personal serviert die Mahlzeiten, die in der mit Sternenlampen geschmückten Küche zubereitet werden. ✳ **PAGE DE GAUCHE** Entrée de la chambre de Franca bordée de tapis. **CI-DESSUS** Les étoiles des souks de Marrakech et les verres jaunis des fenêtres distillent une lumière dorée dans cette salle de bains. **DOUBLE PAGE SUIVANTE** Préparés sous le ciel étoilé de la cuisine, les plats sont servis par un personnel en habit traditionnel.

DAR MOULAY BOUBKER

MARRAKESH

The restoration of this Moroccan palace
expresses one man's passion for a magical city.

There may be a hidden meaning to the swimming pool, at the bottom of which the Greek god Hermes, guide to travellers, contemplates the tree of life.

Xavier Guerrand-Hermès, fit descendant of a family that has always loved Marrakesh, has restored a palace here that is typical of the stately buildings of 17th century Morocco. In the old days, Dar Moulay Boubker – the name of the palace – formed a complex of harem, patio, reception rooms on the ground floor and private apartments on the first floor. It is hard to imagine that only recently the floors here were still of beaten earth, and the beams and plasterwork in the last stages of decay. Authenticity applies, as in seats encrusted with mother-of-pearl, furniture from Baghdad, and a noble Persian tapestry shot with gold thread. A final detail: the palace is very close to the Sidi-Bel-Abbès mosque. Not by chance, perhaps, since Xavier Guerrand-Hermès is an acknowledged specialist in comparative religion. *Mektoub*, it is written, as they say in Arabic.

Koketterie oder sanfter Spott? Am Grund des Swimmingpools beherrscht der griechische Gott Hermes, der Begleiter der Wanderer und Reisenden, einen Baum des Lebens.

Was Xavier Guerrand-Hermès mit diesem Bild auch im Sinn gehabt haben mag – als treuer Nachfahre einer Familie, die der Stadt Marrakesch seit langem verbunden ist, ließ er einen Palast restaurieren, der die marokkanischen Herrschaftsresidenzen des 17. Jahrhunderts beispielhaft repräsentiert. Zuvor bestand der Palast Dar Moulay Boubker aus einem Harem, einem Patio, Empfangsräumen im Parterre und Privatgemächern auf der ersten Etage. Man kann sich kaum vorstellen, dass diese Böden noch bis vor kurzem aus gestampftem Lehm bestanden und störendes Gebälk oder Stuck in diesen Räumen zu verfallen drohten. Die Einrichtung ist hingegen authentisch, wie die syrischen Stühle mit ihren Perlmuttintarsien, die Möbel aus Bagdad und der mit Goldfäden gearbeitete persische Wandteppich aus dem 17. Jahrhundert. Ein letztes Detail: Der Palast liegt in unmittelbarer Nähe der Sidi-Bel-Abbes-Moschee. Reiner Zufall? Xavier Guerrand-Hermès ist ein anerkannter Experte auf dem Gebiet der Vergleichenden Religionswissenschaft. *Mektoub*, sagt man auf Arabisch: »So steht es geschrieben«.

Coquetterie ou sens de la dérision? C'est au fond de la piscine que le dieu grec Hermès, guide des voyageurs, domine un arbre de vie.

N'importe ce sens caché, c'est en fidèle descendant d'une famille attachée à Marrakech depuis longtemps que Xavier Guerrand-Hermès a restauré un palais typique des nobles bâtiments marocains du 17ᵉ siècle. Autrefois, Dar Moulay Boubker, c'est le nom du palais, formait un ensemble partagé entre le harem, le patio, les pièces de réception au rez-de-chaussée et les appartements privés à l'étage. Difficile d'imaginer que les sols étaient récemment encore en terre battue; impossible d'envisager que les poutres, ou les plâtres, agonisaient ici. L'authenticité s'applique encore au mobilier avec ces chaises syriennes incrustées de nacre, ces meubles de Bagdad, ou encore cette tapisserie perse du 17ᵉ siècle, cousue de fils d'or. Dernier détail: le palais est situé tout près de la mosquée Sidi-Bel-Abbès. Hasard des destinées? Xavier Guerrand-Hermès est un spécialiste reconnu de l'histoire comparée des religions. *Mektoub*, c'était écrit, dit-on en arabe.

※ **FACING PAGE AND ABOVE** A low table with a mosaic top and marble armchairs from India match the nobility of the 17th century patio. ※ **LINKE SEITE UND OBEN** Dieser niedrige Tisch mit der Mosaikplatte sowie die indischen Marmorsessel tragen zur edlen Wirkung des Patios aus dem 17. Jahrhundert bei. ※ **PAGE DE GAUCHE ET CI-DESSUS** Table basse au plateau en mosaïque et fauteuils indiens en marbre s'accordent à la noblesse du patio 17e.

❋ **FACING PAGE** The first floor salon opens on the swimming pool, through the door to the left. A panorama by Dufour lit by 19th century Moroccan lanterns. **ABOVE** Syrian mother-of-pearl encrusted furniture is a feature throughout the house. On the commode with its Bedouin clock, Moroccan jewelry. ❋ **LINKE SEITE** Die rechte Tür im Salon auf der ersten Etage führt zum Swimmingpool. Marokkanische Lampen aus dem 19. Jahrhundert beleuchten eine Panorama-tapete von Dufour. **OBEN** Exemplare dieses mit Perlmuttintarsien verzierten syrischen Mobiliars sind über das ganze Gebäude verteilt. Auf der Kommode eine beduinische Standuhr und marokkanischer Schmuck. ❋ **PAGE DE GAUCHE** Le salon de l'étage s'ouvre sur la piscine par la porte de droite. Un papier panora-mique de Dufour est éclairci par des lanternes marocaines du 19e siècle. **CI-DESSUS** Le mobilier syrien incrusté de nacre est une constante dans la maison. Sur la commode dotée d'une horloge à la bédouine, des bijoux marocains.

❊ **ABOVE** The work of Marrakesh artisans – *zelligs* on the walls and floors, painted and carved wood – is stunningly beautiful. **PAGES 48-47** Abdelghani Benkirane, a specialist in restoration, oversaw the work for three years. ❊ **OBEN** Die Handwerksarbeiten von Marrakesch – *zelliges* an Wänden und Böden, Holzmalerei und -schnitzerei – sind überwältigend in ihrer Pracht. **SEITE 48-47** Abdelghani Benkirane, ein Restaurationsexperte, überwachte drei Jahre lang die Arbeiten. ❊ **CI-DESSUS** Le travail des artisans de Marrakech – zelliges qui habillent murs ou sols, bois peints ou sculptés –, est étourdissant de beauté. **PAGES 48-47** Un spécialiste de la restauration, Abdelghani Benkirane, a veillé pendant trois années aux travaux.

✳ **ABOVE** The terrace surrounding the patio offers a superb view of the medina and minaret of the Sidi-Bel-Abbès mosque. And – luxury of luxuries – the tower has an elevator. ✳ **OBEN** Die Terrasse, die den Patio einfasst, bietet eine herrliche Aussicht auf die Medina und das Minarett der Sidi-Bel-Abbes-Moschee. Außerordentlich luxuriös ist auch der Aufzug im ehemaligen Wehrturm. ✳ **CI-DESSUS** La terrasse entourant le patio offre une vue splendide sur la médina et le minaret de la mosquée Sidi-Bel-Abbès. Comble de luxe, la tour de guet abrite désormais un ascenseur.

Dar Badi
ASILAH

The view of the Atlantic from this house on the rampart is as good as it gets.

Confronted with the elements, sometimes furious and sometimes at peace, the owners of this former fisherman's house have banished all trace of clutter which might interfere with the view. Limpidity can be a deliberate decorative choice.

The pure white walls will only bear the thinnest of coloured stripes; the furniture is pared to a minimum, with nothing but banquettes and sofas made by local craftsmen for collapsing on when it's too hot outside. The overwhelming décor here is the sea. The owners are specialists, and they know nothing can upstage nature. The architect Charles Chauliaguet raised this house to its present height, given that it was partly built inside the 6 foot thick medina walls. Organized around a patio with a hundred-year-old fig tree, the original low construction was nothing more than a single large and lightless room. Today, with two floors atop along with plenty of window apertures and terraces linked by walkways, the house has a contemporary air without belying its origins. This is Northern Morocco inspired by the Mediterranean of antiquity. Here even Ithacan Ulysses might have come to approve the sunset over the wine-dark Atlantic.

Die Besitzer dieses Fischerhauses haben angesichts der mal harmlosen, mal entfesselten Elemente alles Überflüssige, jeden Blickfang in ihren Räumen vermieden. Das Haus ist durchgehend klar und nüchtern gestaltet und wirkt beinahe keusch.

Das strahlende Weiß der Wände wird nur an den Durchgängen durch ganz schmale Farbstreifen gebrochen. Die Möblierung ist entsprechend sparsam, doch laden mehrere Sofas und Bänke, die von den Handwerkern der Umgebung gefertigt wurden, zu Ruhepausen während der heißen Tage ein. Der eigentliche Schmuck des Hauses ist das Meer, denn die Besitzer sind der Überzeugung, dass die Natur als Dekoration nicht zu überbieten sei. Der Architekt Charles Chauliaguet hat das Haus, das zum Teil in die 1,80 m starken Befestigungsmauern der Medina gebaut war, nach allen Regeln der Kunst aufgestockt. Das vorhandene untere Bauwerk, das um einen Patio und einen hundertjährigen Feigenbaum angelegt war, war kaum mehr als ein großer, stets schattiger Raum. Nun, nachdem es mit zwei weiteren lichtdurchfluteten Stockwerken überbaut worden ist, mit Terrassen, die durch Stege miteinander verbunden sind, weht ein Hauch von Zeitgeist durch das Haus, ohne dass es seinen Ursprung verleugnete. Angeblich ist der marokkanische Norden von der mediterranen Antike inspiriert. Hier aber genießen Penelope und Odysseus allabendlich gemeinsam den Sonnenuntergang auf den silbergesäumten Fluten des Atlantiks.

Face aux éléments, tantôt apaisés, tantôt déchaînés, les propriétaires de cette maison de pêcheurs ont banni le fouillis où pourrait se perdre le regard. La limpidité est un choix en décoration, un vœu de chasteté en somme.

Les murs, d'une blancheur immaculée, ne tolèrent que de fines rayures posées sur les passages. Point trop de mobilier, juste des banquettes et des canapés réalisés par les artisans des environs et où l'on peut s'alanguir les jours de grande chaleur. Au fond, le vrai décor, c'est la mer. Les propriétaires, en spécialistes, savent bien qu'il n'y a pas plus décoratif que la nature elle-même. L'architecte Charles Chauliaguet a surélevé dans les règles de l'art une maison en partie édifiée à l'intérieur des remparts de la médina (dont l'épaisseur est de 1,80 m!). Organisée autour d'un patio et du figuier centenaire, cette construction basse n'était qu'une grande pièce plongée dans la pénombre. Surélevée de deux étages, percée de part en part d'ouvertures, ses terrasses reliées par des passerelles, elle est traversée par un souffle contemporain sans renier ses origines. On se dit ainsi que le Nord marocain s'inspire de la Méditerranée antique. Mais ici Pénélope et Ulysse jouissent ensemble, chaque soir, d'un soleil qui se couche sur des flots ourlés d'argent de l'Atlantique.

❋ **PREVIOUS PAGES** As the waves break against the ramparts below, the owners savor the success of their project. **ABOVE** The world is blue, seen from this fisherman's house where meals are taken under a white awning. Every evening the sun sets directly in front. You can view it from terrace or walkway – the choice is yours. ❋ **VORHERGEHENDE DOPPELSEITE** Wenn die Wellen sich unterhalb der Befestigungsanlage brechen, genießen die Hausbewohner ihr Meisterwerk. **OBEN** Von diesem Fischerhaus aus, unter dem Sonnenschutz aus Segeltuch, scheint die ganze Welt in Blau getaucht. Allabendlich bietet sich hier das Schauspiel des Sonnenuntergangs, das man nach Belieben von der Terrasse oder vom Steg aus beobachten kann. ❋ **DOUBLE PAGE PRECEDENTE** Tandis que les vagues se brisent sous les remparts, les propriétaires de la maison savourent la réussite de leur projet. **CI-DESSUS** Le monde est bleu depuis cette maison de pêcheurs où l'on se restaure à l'abri d'un taud blanc. Chaque soir, le soleil se couche juste en face. En terrasse ou sur la passerelle, c'est au choix pour le spectateur.

✳ **ABOVE** The owners reject the Pierre Loti style as "neo-colonist orientalism", preferring to show nothing but furniture and objects made in the Rif region. "We've done our best to fit in", they say. ✳ **OBEN** Die Eigentümer halten nichts vom »Pierre-Loti-Stil«, von neokolonialistischem Orientalismus. Sie dekorieren ihr Haus lieber mit Möbeln und Produkten aus der Umgebung des Rifgebirges. »Wir haben uns alle Mühe gegeben, uns zu integrieren«, lautet vielmehr ihre Philosophie. ✳ **CI-DESSUS** Les propriétaires rejettent «le style Pierre Loti», «cet orientalisme néocolonialiste», pour n'exposer dans la maison que des meubles ou objets fabriqués dans la région du Rif. «Nous avons fait de notre mieux pour nous intégrer», philosophent-ils.

❋ **BELOW** In the starkly decorated bedrooms, simple furniture in harmony with the holiday atmosphere. Thus the Moroccan North acquires a dash of the Mediterranean. ❋ **UNTEN** In den mönchisch kargen Zimmern passt sich die schlichte Möblierung dem Stil eines Ferienortes an. Der marokkanische Norden gibt sich hier mediterran. ❋ **CI-DESSOUS** Dans les chambres monacales, un mobilier simple s'harmonise au décor balnéaire. Le Nord marocain prend ainsi des allures méditerranéennes.

※ **ABOVE** The green bedroom has a toilet area with a basin and a looking glass fashioned from *zelligs*. **BELOW** In the big blue bedroom, the masonry banquettes (*doukana*) are covered with fabrics of the kind worn by women of the Rif (*fouta*) and thin woolen blankets (*haik*). ※ **OBEN** Im grünen Zimmer gibt es eine Waschgelegenheit mit einem Waschbecken und einem mit *zelliges* verkleideten Spiegel. **UNTEN** Im weiträumigen blauen Zimmer bedecken Gewebe (*fouta*), die auch die Frauen des Rif tragen, und Decken aus feinem Leinen (*haïk*) die gemauerten Bänke (*doukana*). ※ **CI-DESSUS** La chambre verte dispose d'un coin toilette avec un lavabo et un miroir façonnés de zelliges. **CI-DESSOUS** Dans la grande chambre bleue, les banquettes en maçonnerie (*doukana*) sont recouvertes d'étoffes portées par les femmes du Rif (*fouta*) et de couvertures de laine fine (*haïk*).

Dar Karma
ASILAH

Above, immaculate low walls;
below, a lively patio around a fig tree with secret ramifications.

The door opens. The Atlantic is no more than a distant murmur, though there's a salty tang in the air. The wind ripples under the women's veils.

The door closes and the sea is heard no more. The white building shelters the people in it from the sun and the sea. Everyone is resting. Dar Karma, the house of the fig tree, is near Tangier, and it's a haven of peace for anyone who visits. Your first steps inside are taken on the patio of Fez brick. You stop by the big tree, which seems to root the entire house deep in the ground. In front is a building with three stories – traditionally constructed, but enriched by the cunning of the architect Charles Chauliaguet, it rises room by room, from salon to terrace, each a new enticement to migrate to Asilah. A few days is all it takes. At this end of Africa, a traveller can easily lose his bearings and forget the way back North. The owners are collectors of Nigerian Igbo sculptures and oil lamps from Mali, and they've left their treasures around the house. In sunshine or stormy weather, this is a wonderful place to be.

Wir öffnen die Tür. Aus der Ferne klingt der Atlantik nur mehr wie ein leises Murmeln, aber der unverwechselbare Meeresgeruch hängt weiter in der Luft. Der Wind bringt ihn mit, dieser Wind, der sich unter die Schleier der Frauen schleicht.

Als wir die Tür schließen, gibt die Natur Ruhe. Das weiße Gebäude schützt seine Bewohner vor der glühenden Sonne und dem tosenden Meer. Dar Karma, das Feigenbaum-Haus, liegt in der Nähe von Tanger, ein wahrer Hafen der Ruhe. Als erstes erspüren die Fußsohlen Ziegel aus Fes, den Bodenbelag im Patio. Am Feigenbaum legt man eine Pause ein, zumal der große Baum die Verzweigungen des Hauses widerzuspiegeln scheint. Der traditionelle Bau hat drei Stockwerke, die von Raum zu Raum, von den Salons zu den Terrassen in die Höhe steigen – eine Einladung zum Schlendern. Der Architekt Charles Chauliaguet hat auch hier sein Können unter Beweis gestellt. An dieser Spitze Afrikas verliert man die Orientierung. Liegt es am Seewind? Das Haus bezeugt eine Offenheit gegenüber dem schwarzen Kontinent, wie die Skulpturen der Igbo aus Nigeria beweisen, oder die Öllampen aus Mali – die Besitzer sind selbst Sammler. Das Wetter soll schlechter werden? Kein Problem – für die Bewohner von Dar Karma scheint immer die Sonne.

Poussons la porte. Au loin, l'Atlantique n'est plus qu'un lointain murmure. Demeure cette tenace odeur d'iode. Ce vent qui s'enroule sous le voile des femmes.

Refermons la porte. La nature ne gémit plus. La bâtisse blanche abrite son monde des fureurs solaires et marines. Tout le monde se repose. Dar Karma, la maison du figuier, située à proximité de Tanger, est un havre de paix pour ses visiteurs. Les pieds foulent d'abord les briquettes de Fez du patio. Un arrêt s'impose à proximité du grand arbre, lequel semble répartir les ramifications de l'édifice. Apparaissent le bâtiment et ses trois niveaux. De construction traditionnelle, mais enrichi du savoir de l'architecte Charles Chauliaguet, l'ensemble s'élève de nids en nids, de salons en terrasses, véritables invites à des migrations minuscules. Quelques jours suffisent pour s'égarer. Au bout de cette Afrique, les voyageurs perdent le Nord. Est-ce le vent du large? La maison est ouverte au continent noir avec, ici, de filiformes sculptures Igbo du Nigeria, et là, des lampes à huile du Mali introduits par les propriétaires-collectioneurs. Le temps se gâte? Impossible au creux du nid. Dans les yeux des habitants de Dar Karma, le regard est toujours bleu.

❊ **LEFT** Set in the white façade, door and shutter form a microcosm of the building's beauty. **BELOW** The door opens on the patio with its *bejmat* surface (bricks from Fez). This square courtyard with its spreading fig tree is open to the ground floor rooms, each with its cedar wood door. **FACING PAGE** A *zelligs* table (made with tiny chips of enamel tiles) for serving mint tea. ❊ **LINKS** An der weißen Fassade bilden Tür und Fensterladen ein schönes Ensemble. **UNTEN** Direkt hinter der beschlagenen Tür liegt der Patio, der mit *bejmat* (Ziegeln aus Fes) ausgelegt ist. Von dem quadratischen Platz mit dem mächtigen Feigenbaum gehen die Zimmer im Parterre ab. Jedes hat eine Tür aus Zedernholz. **RECHTE SEITE** Ein mit *zelliges* (winzige Scherben glasierter Ziegel) verzierter Tisch – hier wird der Pfefferminztee serviert. ❊ **A GAUCHE** Sur la façade blanche porte et volet forment un calice à la beauté de l'édifice. **CI-DESSOUS** Il suffit de pousser la porte cloutée pour découvrir le patio et fouler le sol en *bejmat* (briquettes de Fez). Depuis ce carré dominé par l'imposant figuier, on pénètre dans les pièces du rez-de-chaussée toutes abritées de portes en cèdre. **PAGE DE DROITE** Une table en zelliges (éclats de briques émaillées taillés en minuscules morceaux), pour servir le thé à la menthe.

❋ **ABOVE** A bedroom, with a sofa that serves as a bed. **RIGHT** Wooden chair and desk made of wood cut and bleached by craftsmen in the Asilah souk. **FACING PAGE** The white salon with its décor of African masks is bathed in soft light from pierced terracotta sconces. ❋ **OBEN** Eines der Zimmer mit einem Diwan, der auch als Bett dient. **RECHTS** Stuhl und Schreibtisch aus ausgesägtem und gebleichtem Holz, aus einer Werkstatt im Souk von Asilah. **RECHTE SEITE** Der weiße Salon mit den afri-kanischen Masken wird durch die durchbrochenen Terrakottalampen in ein weiches Licht getaucht. ❋ **CI-DESSOUS** Une chambre et son divan qui fait office de lit. **A DROITE** Chaise et bureau en bois découpés et blanchis par les artisans du souk d'Asilah. **PAGE DE DROITE** Dominé par des masques africains, le salon blanc est tamisé par des appliques en terre cuite ajourée et blanchie.

Dar EL Hanna

Essaouira

The owner of this house has made the utmost of a limited space
filled with secret corners.

A hippie rendezvous in the early 1970s and Orson Welles's playground when he was filming "Othello", Essaouira has long attracted artists, writers and fashion people.

Without directly belonging to this tribe, Geneviève Canet and Joël Martial discovered the region in the early 1990s. They were enchanted by the hospitality of the local people and the magnificence of the landscapes, and a year later they bought a village house nearby. It was a ruin, and anyway much too small, everybody said. But what a surprise for the begrudgers! The place has metamorphosed into a charming retreat. Ever since the beaten earth of the patio gave way to checkerboard slabs and the terrace walls were covered in pinkish lime wash to go with its cement tiles, the visitors have stopped sneering. In essence, the house has lost nothing of its original structure. Facing the patio, a kitchen-living room leads through to a bedroom. Upstairs, the terrace opens onto two small bedrooms. The argan wood furniture, designed by Joël Martial, is the work of a local carpenter.

Essaouira, Anfang der 1970er Jahre ein berühmter Hippie-Ort, wo sich Orson Welles zur Zeit seines Othello-Erfolges vergnügte, zieht seit vielen Jahren Künstler, Schriftsteller und Modemacher an.

Geneviève Canet und Joël Martial gehören zwar nicht direkt zu dieser Szene, als sie die Gegend jedoch Anfang der 1990er Jahre entdeckten, waren sie von der Gastfreundschaft der Einheimischen und der großartigen Landschaft so begeistert, dass sie ein Jahr später in der Umgebung ein Haus kauften. Mit seiner bescheidenen Fassade in einem kleinen Dorf war es zunächst kein Prunkstück. Zweifler, die es kritisch als Ruine oder Zwergenhäuschen bezeichnet hatten, wurden spätestens eines Besseren belehrt, als der schlichte Lehmboden im Patio sich in ein schwarzweißes Schachbrett verwandelt hatte. Die gekalkten Mauern, die auf der Terrasse rosa getüncht sind, überzeugen ebenso wie der Fliesenbelag aus Zement. Trotzdem ist die ursprüngliche Bauweise noch zu erkennen. Vor dem Patio liegt ein großes Wohnzimmer, eine Kombination aus Salon und Küche, das in einen weiteren Raum führt. Im ersten Stock grenzt eine Terrasse an zwei kleine Zimmer. Die Möbel aus Arganholz wurden nach einem Entwurf von Joël Martial in einer Schreinerei vor Ort angefertigt.

Cité hippie au début des années 1970, terrain de jeu d'Orson Welles à l'époque de son Othello, Essaouira attire depuis longtemps artistes, écrivains et gens de mode.

Sans directement appartenir à la tribu, Geneviève Canet et Joël Martial découvrent la région au début des années 1990. Séduits par l'hospitalité du cru et la magnificence des paysages, ils achètent une année plus tard une maison des environs. À l'origine modeste façade au cœur d'un humble village, l'endroit se mue en refuge de charme. Quelle surprise pour ses contempteurs! Une ruine, disaient les uns, un mouchoir de poche, prétendaient les autres. Mais, depuis que la terre battue qui couvrait le patio a été reléguée aux oubliettes, qu'à la place un damier noir et blanc joue à la marelle, que les murs passés à la chaux, teintés en rose sur la terrasse, amusent des carrelages de ciment, eh bien, les visiteurs ne badinent plus. Fondamentalement, la maison n'a pas perdu sa structure originelle. Devant le patio, une salle de séjour à la fois salon et cuisine borde une chambre; à l'étage, une terrasse s'ouvre sur deux petites chambres. Le mobilier en bois d'argan, dessiné par Joël Martial, est l'œuvre d'un menuisier local.

✳ **FACING PAGE** The pink staircase leading to the upper floor. **ABOVE** The stools of the house are the work of Joël Martial. In the patio, there's little to do except read, talk – and dread returning to the big city. ✳ **LINKE SEITE** Die rosafarbene Treppe führt in den ersten Stock. **OBEN** Sämtliche Schemel im Haus sind das Werk Joël Martials. Wozu eignet sich der Patio besser als zum Lesen, zum Plaudern … oder um darüber nachzudenken, ob man wirklich in die europäische Großstadt zurückkkehren will? ✳ **PAGE DE GAUCHE** L'escalier rose mène à l'étage. **CI-DESSUS** Les tabourets de la maison sont l'œuvre de Joël Martial. Dans le patio, il n'y a rien d'autre à faire que lire, bavarder … et redouter le retour dans les grandes villes d'Europe.

❋ **ABOVE AND FACING PAGE** After the black and white of the entrance came colours and cement tiles, from the corridors to the lime washed terrace area. The wainscoting of the corridor leading to the living room is made with cement tiles. ❋ **OBEN UND RECHTE SEITE** Auf das Schwarzweiß im Eingang folgen die Zementfliesen und die gekalkten Mauergänge der Terrasse. Auf dem Boden und im unteren Bereich der Wände im Gang zum Salon liegen Zementkacheln. ❋ **CI-DESSUS ET PAGE DE DROITE** Après le noir et blanc de l'entrée, la couleur et les carreaux de ciment prennent le relais, des couloirs aux murs de la terrasse passés à la chaux. Le soubassement du couloir qui mène au salon est fait de carreaux de ciment.

✳ **FACING PAGE AND ABOVE** The masonry banquettes (*doukana*) of the ground floor living room are covered with Indian cushions. The furniture, like this lantern and ironwork table, was made by a local craftsman from sketches by Joël Martial. ✳ **LINKE SEITE UND OBEN** Auf den gemauerten Bänken (*doukana*) im Salon im Erdgeschoss liegen indische Kissen. Die Möbel, wie die Laterne und der Eisentisch, wurden nach Entwürfen von Joël Martial vor Ort produziert. ✳ **PAGE DE GAUCHE ET CI-DESSUS** Les banquettes en maçonnerie (*doukana*) du salon du rez-de-chaussée sont recouvertes de coussins indiens. Le mobilier, comme cette lanterne et cette table en fer, a été fabriqué par un artisan local d'après les croquis de Joël Martial.

❋ **ABOVE** The kitchen is decorated with utensils from the region. **FACING PAGE** The merest beam of sunshine is caught by the aperture, lighting the limewashed walls and the kitchen sink. The crockery is from Safi. ❋ **OBEN** Die Küche ist nach einheimischer Art eingerichtet. **RECHTE SEITE** Durch diese Öffnung fällt noch der schwächste Sonnenstrahl auf die gekalkten Mauern und das Spülbecken in der Küche. Keramikgeschirr aus Safi. ❋ **CI-DESSUS** La cuisine est décorée d'ustensiles de la région. **PAGE DE DROITE** Le moindre rayon de soleil est capté par cette percée zénithale qui éclaire les murs passés à la chaux et l'évier de la cuisine. Vaisselle de Safi.

Aït Bou Goumez
& Ouarzazate

The Berber buildings in this fortified village have stood for centuries
at the foot of the mountain range.

On either side of the High Atlas, villages built of *pisé* melt into the same background of arid earth dotted with low bushes. The time of *razzias* (raids) is long past, but the defensive architecture so characteristic of the Berbers still remains.

At the first sign of trouble, people, animals and provisions were piled up together in these houses, which were like strongboxes against thieves and bandits. Around Ouarzazate they have several floors, with the ground one reserved for mules, goats and sheep, the first for fodder, the second for the family and the third for an open terrace. The towers on their corners have no windows, only a hole or two just big enough for a gun barrel to poke through. Life was and still is lived in the courtyards below, where there is plenty of light and fresh air. These *pisé* houses, constantly gouged by rain and eternally under reconstruction, radiate a sense of both strength and fragility. The spirit of the people here is still wedded to the soil. Time has left deep marks on their faces, and they've stood up to so much harsh weather they can defy the world. Only the mention of djinns, the evil spirits of their legends, can make them shudder – but not for long. A shrug, a prayer…and they go back to their fields again.

Auf beiden Seiten des Hohen Atlas verschmelzen die Lehmdörfer mit der trockenen, überall von Buschwerk durchsetzten Landschaft. Die Zeiten kriegerischer Auseinandersetzungen und Razzien sind vorbei, doch die wehrhafte Architektur der Berber blieb erhalten.

In den Behausungen drängen sich Menschen und Vieh; auch die Vorräte sind dort untergebracht. In der Gegend um Ouarzazate stehen mehrstöckige Bauten, deren Erdgeschoss den Maultieren, Ziegen und Schafen vorbehalten ist. Die erste Etage dient als Speicher, auf der zweiten wohnt die Familie, während das dritte Stockwerk die Terrasse bildet. Die schlanken Ecktürme haben keine Fenster sondern nur Schießscharten, durch die gerade ein Gewehrlauf passt. Das Leben spielt sich im lichten, luftigen Hof ab. Diese Lehmbauten, die ständig vom Regen ausgewaschen und genauso oft wieder aufgebaut werden, wirken fragil und robust zugleich. Die Menschen, die bereits so viele Unbilden erlitten haben, bieten der Welt trotzig die Stirn. Die Zeit hinterlässt tiefe Spuren in den Gesichtern. Es ist nicht leicht, den Dorfbewohnern Furcht einzujagen, es sei denn, man erwähnt einen Dschinn, einen bösen Geist aus alten Geschichten. Aber auch das hält nicht lange vor – schon zucken sie mit den Schultern, sprechen ein Gebet … und kehren aufs Feld zurück.

Des deux côtés du Haut Atlas, les villages en pisé se confondent avec la terre aride parsemée de buissons. Le temps des rixes et des razzias est loin, mais l'architecture défensive, caractéristique des constructions berbères, demeure.

Les hommes, le bétail et les provisions s'entassent dans les habitations, sorte de coffre-fort à la mode tribale. Autour de Ouarzazate, elles disposent de plusieurs niveaux avec un rez-de-chaussée réservé aux mulets, chèvres et moutons; un premier étage qui fait office de grenier, un deuxième réservé à la famille, et un dernier niveau en guise de terrasse. Sur les tours élancées qui ornent les angles, pas de fenêtres, juste une ouverture pour laisser passer le canon d'un fusil. La vie se passe dans la cour qui apporte air et lumière. De ces maisons en pisé, ravinées par la pluie, éternellement rebâties, émane un sentiment de fragilité et de puissance à la fois. L'âme des habitants est restée près de la terre. Les corps ont résisté à tant d'intempéries qu'ils peuvent bien défier le monde. Sur les visages, le temps a laissé des traces profondes. Seule l'évocation des djinns, ces esprits malins des contes, peut effrayer les villageois. Mais pas longtemps. Un haussement d'épaule, quelques prières … et ils repartent aux champs.

※ **ABOVE AND FACING PAGE** The common room in a house in the valley of Aït Bou Goumez. Coloured motifs characterize a space which changes constantly all through the day. The colours also have a way of warming the place in winter, which is otherwise icy cold. ※ **OBEN UND RECHTE SEITE** Gemeinschaftsraum eines Hauses im Tal von Aït Bou Goumez. Bunte Muster zieren den Raum, der sich im Laufe des Tages ständig verändert. Die Farben bringen Wärme an diesen im Winter eisigen Ort. ※ **CI-DESSUS ET PAGE DE DROITE** Pièce commune d'une maison de la vallée de Aït Bou Goumez. Des motifs colorés habillent un espace qui se transforme tout au long de la journée. Les couleurs réchauffent un habitat glacial en hiver.

✳ **ABOVE AND RIGHT** Doors carved according to the canons of Berber art are becoming rarer. The rural exodus has led to the disappearance of many craftsmen, and people repair the ravages of time as best they can, with scrap metal if need be. ✳ **OBEN UND RECHTS** Solche Türen, die allen Regeln der Berberkunst entsprechen, werden immer seltener. Aufgrund der Landflucht gibt es immer weniger Handwerker, sodass die witterungsbedingten Schäden mehr schlecht als recht repariert werden. ✳ **CI-DESSUS ET À DROITE** De plus en plus rares sont les portes sculptées selon les canons de l'art berbère. L'exode rural conduit à la disparition des artisans et l'on répare comme on peut les outrages du temps, c'est-à-dire avec des bidons métalliques.

❋ **ABOVE** At Aït Benhaddou, wheat, barley, millet and maize formed the staple diet of the Berbers. The sideboard with its battery of cooking pots occupies most of the kitchen. **FOLLOWING PAGES** General view of Aït Benhaddou. **OBEN** Grundnahrungsmittel der Berber sind Weizen, Gerste, Hirse und Mais. Hier sieht man die Küche, die im Wesentlichen aus der Anrichte und einer Ansammlung von Töpfen besteht. **FOLGENDE DOPPELSEITE** Gesamtansicht von Aït Benhaddou. ❋ **CI-DESSUS** À Aït Benhaddou, le blé, l'orge, le millet et le maïs constituent la nourriture de base des Berbères. Le buffet et sa batterie de marmites occupent l'essentiel de la cuisine. **DOUBLE PAGE SUIVANTE** Vue générale de Aït Benhaddou.

Dar En Nadour

Dar Djellouli

TUNISIA

Dar en Nadour

Sidi Bou Saïd

To visit this house with the blue Mediterranean spread before it,
is to follow in the footsteps of Henri Matisse.

From the terrace, the view offers an inexhaustible source of Mediterranean nuance, dominated by a subtle shifting quality of blue that lingers in the memory.

The owners of Dar en Nadour still remember Henri Matisse sitting on their terrace, painting. It's a place of deep serenity. For generations the vine-clad house behind has been giving of itself to all comers. With a décor veering from the West to the Orient and back again, it is filled with sofas, poufs and cushions, along with a collection registered as part of Tunisia's national heritage with the ministry of culture. Among the masterpieces here are a couple of large Roman mosaics, sculptures of animals, and numerous busts and statues from antiquity. Corridors and walls of enamelled tiles (14th century Spanish-Moorish *zliss* or *zelligs*) lead through to cool, often windowless rooms; in the heat of the day, shade is more to be valued than any panorama, no matter how unique. At sunset, a light breeze caresses the fronds of the palm tree.

Von der Terrasse aus bietet sich eine umwerfende Aussicht auf die stets wechselnden Farbnuancen des Mittelmeers mit seinem feinen changierenden Blauton.

Die Eigentümer können sich noch daran erinnern, wie Henri Matisse auf eben dieser Terrasse gemalt hat. Allein, dass der Maler hier residierte, spricht für die heitere Ausstrahlung des Ortes. Das mit Weinreben berankte Haus beherbergt seit Generationen Gäste. Wie eine sinnliche Verbindung von Orient und Okzident quillt es über vor Sofas, Kissen und gepolsterten Hockern, damit es niemandem an einer Sitzgelegenheit mangele. Hier findet sich auch eine beeindruckende Sammlung, die beim tunesischen Kultusministerium verzeichnet ist. Eine kleine Auswahl: zwei echte große römische Mosaiken, außerdem antike Tierskulpturen, Statuen und Büsten. Über Fliesen aus *zliss* oder *zelliges* im spanisch-maurischen Stil des 14. Jahrhunderts gleitet man in die angrenzenden kühlen fensterlosen Räume. Wenn es richtig heiß ist, siegt die Sehnsucht nach Schatten über die Freude am Panoramablick, auch wenn dieser einmalig ist. Abends streicht eine sanfte Brise durch die Palmblätter.

Depuis la terrasse, la vue est une source inépuisable de nuances méditerranéennes où domine un bleu subtil et changeant. Reflet de la mer dans le ciel, la couleur éblouit et se fixe dans les mémoires.

Les propriétaires se souviennent encore du peintre Henri Matisse peignant ici. La présence du maître suffit à attester la force sereine de l'endroit. Recouverte de vigne, la maison reçoit, donne, et ce depuis des générations. Dédale sensuel entre Orient et Occident, elle déborde de sofas, poufs et coussins pour accueillir son monde. On ne peut manquer une collection impressionnante inscrite au patrimoine du ministère tunisien de la Culture. Pièces de choix: deux grandes mosaïques authentiquement romaines, des sculptures d'animaux, des statues et des bustes antiques. Parmi les carreaux peints, ces *zliss* ou zelliges de style hispano-mauresque du 14ᵉ siècle, on glisse dans les pièces fraîches parfois sans fenêtres. C'est qu'aux heures chaudes, l'ombre a plus de valeur qu'un panorama, même si il est unique. En fin de journée, un vent léger caresse les feuilles de palmier.

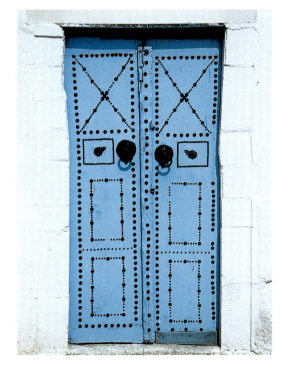

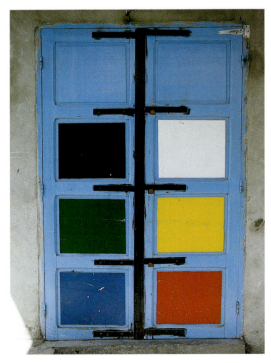

✳ **FACING PAGE** A collection of valuable glasses and decanters. **ABOVE** After the patio, the long vestibule contains a collection of opalines, glass, and old Arab perfume bottles against a background of earthenware tiles. ✳ **LINKE SEITE** Eine bemerkenswerte Sammlung wertvoller Gläser und Karaffen. **OBEN** Der Vorraum hinter dem Patio beherbergt eine Opalglas-Sammlung, Glaswaren und alte Flakons mit arabischem Parfüm vor Fayencehintergrund. ✳ **PAGE DE GAUCHE** Une collection de verres précieux et des carafes retiennent l'attention. **CI-DESSOUS** Après le patio, le long vestibule abrite une collection d'opalines, de verreries et de vieux flacons de parfum arabe sur fond de faïence.

❀ **FACING PAGE AND BELOW** The *zliss* (enamelled earthenware tiles) of the small salon and dining room are of the same type as those at the Alhambra in Granada. On the bed of the Dey (governor), the kilims echo the geometry of the tiles. This is a cool place, often used for siestas. **FOLLOWING PAGES** Turquoise wooden panels and *zliss* floors in the magnificent bathroom with its traditional taps and fixtures. ❀ **LINKE SEITE UND UNTEN** Die *zliss* (glasierte Fayencefliesen) im kleinen Salon und im Esszimmer sind in dem gleichen spanisch-maurischen Stil gehalten wie in der Alhambra von Granada. Die Kelims auf dem Bett des Dey, des Gouverneurs, nehmen das geometrische Muster der Fliesen auf. Hier im Kühlen wird Siesta gehalten. **FOLGENDE DOPPELSEITE** Türkisfarbene Täfelung und mit *zliss* verkleidete Böden schmücken das prächtige Bad mit den traditionell angehauchten Armaturen. ❀ **PAGE DE GAUCHE ET CI-DESSOUS** Les *zliss* (carreaux de faïence émaillée) du petit salon et de la salle à manger témoignent du style hispano-mauresque tel qu'on peut l'admirer à l'Alhambra de Grenade. Sur le lit du Dey (gouverneur), les kilims répondent à la géométrie des carrelages. C'est ici qu'on fait la sieste, à la fraîche. **DOUBLE PAGE SUIVANTE** Boiseries turquoise et sols de *zliss* pour la splendide salle de bains avec sa robinetterie d'inspiration traditionnelle.

✻ **ABOVE** A bedroom with the traditinal wooden alcove and 18th century motifs. On the side table, a Louis XV clock. **FACING PAGE** The Louis XV mirrors overlooking the Arab salon reflect the light shed by a Venetian chandelier. Chiselled plaster arabesques and a three-part banquette. ✻ **OBEN** Ein traditioneller hölzerner Alkoven mit Motiven aus dem 18. Jahrhundert schmückt dieses Zimmer. Auf dem hochbeinigen Tisch steht eine Standuhr im Louis-XV-Stil. **RECHTE SEITE** Spiegel im Louis-XV-Stil beherrschen den arabischen Salon und reflektieren das Licht des venezianischen Lüsters. Arabesken aus Stuck und eine dreiteilige Bank. ✻ **CI-DESSUS** Une chambre ornée de la traditionnelle alcôve en bois aux motifs 18ᵉ. Sur la commode, une pendule Louis XV. **PAGE DE DROITE** Des miroirs Louis XV dominent le salon arabe et reflètent les lumières du lustre vénitien. Arabesques de plâtre ciselé et banquette en trois pièces.

✳ **ABOVE AND FACING PAGE** In the salon, which is completely encircled by stucco, are photographs and decorations presented by the state to Ahmed Djellouli's distinguished forebears (photo facing page), who have been prominent Tunisian citizens and ministers for three centuries past. ✳ **OBEN UND RECHTE SEITE** In dem stuckverzierten Salon hängen Fotos und die gesammelten Auszeichnungen der Großeltern von Ahmed Djellouli (auf dem Foto auf der rechten Seite), Notabeln und Minister der letzten drei Jahrhunderte. ✳ **CI-DESSUS ET PAGE DE DROITE** Dans le salon cerclé de stuc, photos et récompenses glanées par les aïeuls d'Ahmed Djellouli (en photo page de droite), notables et ministres depuis trois siècles.

Hammamet

Hidden behind the high walls of Tunisia's Saint-Tropez are a number of traditionally-designed, originally-decorated villas like this one.

You're lost in a maze of streets, with something new and amazing round every corner. Carved and studded doorways of varnished wood open to show clusters of pink and mauve flowers cascading over the immaculate walls beyond.

At the end of a narrow alley, a chink offers a glimpse of a patio in which the interplay of plants and stones echoes the geometry of tiles and arches. Tropical scents float around you as you push open the door with its fish and hand motifs. Welcome to the home of Pierre Pes, a traveller and aesthete who, following the example of Violette and Jean Henson, the Americans who launched Hammamet in the 1930s, has given orientalism fresh impetus with a style all in white. You may well ask, what exactly is a foreign-based aesthete looking for? A moment's hesitation, and the reply comes back: confrontation, influences that might enrich, a clean break, and above all, the illusion of controlling the passage of time. By cheerfully straddling the centuries and surrounding himself with objects passed down by the civilisation of the Moors in Spain, Pierre Pes makes a mockery of the years.

In diesem Wirrwarr der Gassen, das an jeder Ecke neue Überraschungen bereithält, kann man sich hoffnungslos verirren. Die Portale aus lackiertem Holz, mit Nägeln beschlagen und mit Reliefs verziert, erlauben einen Blick auf rosa- und malvenfarbene Blütenstände, die sich über strahlend weiße Mauern ergießen.

Am Ende einer Gasse erspäht man durch einen Türspalt einen Patio, in dem Pflanzen und Steine passend zur Geometrie der Bodenfliesen und Rundbögen arrangiert sind. Ihr tropischer Duft weht auf die Gasse hinaus. Die traditionell mit Nägeln beschlagene Tür zeigt die Fetischmotive Fisch und Hand. Willkommen bei Pierre Pes, dem reisenden Ästheten, der einen rein weißen, orientalisch anmutenden Stil bevorzugt – wie bereits die beiden mondänen Amerikaner Violette und Jean Henson, die Hammamet in den 1930er Jahren zum Aufschwung verhalfen. Die Frage, was dieser anerkannte Schöngeist im Ausland sucht, ist durchaus berechtigt. Ein kurzes Zögern, dann sprudelt die Antwort nur so aus ihm heraus: Konfrontation, bereichernde Einflüsse, Brüche, vor allem aber die Illusion, die Zeit anhalten zu können. Pierre Pes überwindet die Epochengrenzen, indem er sich fröhlich in verschiedenen Jahrhunderten bedient und mit ererbten Gegenständen der spanisch-maurischen Zeit umgibt.

Vous êtes perdu dans un dédale de venelles qui offre à chaque tour et détour son lot d'étonnement. Les portails en bois verni, sculptés et cloutés, laissent transparaître des grappes de fleurs roses, mauves, retombant sur des murs immaculés.

Au bout d'une ruelle, une porte presque close laisse entrevoir l'intérieur d'un patio où l'enchevêtrement des plantes et des pierres répond à la géométrie des carrelages et des arches. Des essences tropicales déferlent jusqu'à vous. Poussez la porte traditionnellement cloutée des motifs fétiches du poisson et de la main. Bienvenue chez Pierre Pes, esthète voyageur qui, à l'instar des très mondains Violette et Jean Henson, ce couple d'Américains qui lança Hammamet dans les années 1930, prolonge l'orientalisme en un style tout de blancheur. Légitimement, vous vous interrogez: que cherche un esthète établi en terre étrangère? Un temps d'hésitation, puis la réponse jaillit: une confrontation, des influences qui pourraient l'enrichir, une rupture et, surtout, l'illusion de maîtriser la fuite du temps. En franchissant allègrement les siècles, en s'entourant d'objets hérités de la civilisation hispano-mauresque, Pierre Pes se rit des époques.

※ **ABOVE, BELOW, FACING PAGE AND FOLLOWING PAGES** Hammamet, which not so long ago was a small village with a shop and a mosque, is now Tunisia's Saint-Tropez. In its small palaces, like the one owned by Pierre Pes shown here, the style is predominantly white, with an antique purity in a place filled with archaeological vestiges left by Carthaginians, Greeks, Romans and Christians. ※ **OBEN, UNTEN, RECHTE SEITE UND FOLGENDE DOPPELSEITEN** Hammamet, das früher nur aus einer Moschee und wenigen Hütten bestand, entwickelte sich zum tunesischen Saint-Tropez. In den kleinen Villen, wie etwa der von Pierre Pes, dominiert die Farbe Weiß in einer antik anmutenden Reinheit – in einer Gegend, die reich ist an archäologischen Funden aus der punischen, griechischen, römischen und christlichen Epoche. ※ **CI-DESSOUS, CI-DESSOUS, PAGE DE DROITE ET DOUBLE PAGES SUIVANTES** Hammamet, qui n'était qu'un petit village avec quelques cases et une mosquée, est devenu le Saint-Tropez de la Tunisie. À l'intérieur des petits palais, comme ici chez Pierre Pes, domine un style tout de blancheur, une pureté antique sur un sol qui recèle des vestiges archéologiques des époques punique, grecque, romaine et chrétienne.

Ghorfas & Troglodytes
Matmata

A visit to a Saharan fortress that continues to hold out against time and a hostile environment.

On the mountains, the *ksour* (fortified village) overlooks the stoney plains of the great Tunisian south. Like giant beehives, its fortified grain stores (*ghorfas* in the Berber language) form complexes of rooms on several levels which are accessible from the outside by stairways.

Ever since the Middle Ages, people in these parts have had to protect themselves from a hostile outside world. For centuries, they were victims of *razzias* (raids); threatened by war, they had no other choice but to protect their precious staples. In this way one of North Africa's greatest architectural curiosities was born of a constant need for security. With its mosque and its school, Matmata has long been a village of cave-dwellers, numbering about a hundred families. In the middle of the last century, the younger generation began to move away to Tunis or migrate to Europe. Today, only a few people are living in the troglodytes, obstinately keeping their distance from the modern world. But they're no longer alone, and far from hostile – because now the troglodyte village has given a brand new possibility to its young. At last they are opening their heavy palm-wood doors to strangers, in the form of tourists, and treating them as friends.

Der *ksour* (eine befestigte Ortschaft) am Berghang thront über den steinigen Ebenen im weiträumigen tunesischen Süden. Die befestigten Speicher (*ghorfas* in der Berbersprache) gleichen riesigen Bienenstöcken und enthalten auf mehreren Etagen ein Geflecht von Räumen, die von außen über Treppen zugänglich sind.

Seit dem Mittelalter schützen sich die hier ansässigen Menschen vor der lebensfeindlichen Außenwelt. Lange Zeit wurden regelmäßig Razzien durchgeführt. Die vom Krieg bedrohten Stämme waren gezwungen, die zum Leben notwendigen Güter zu schützen. Aus dieser allgegenwärtigen Sorge um ihre Sicherheit entstand eine der seltsamsten Architekturformen Nordafrikas. In Matmata, das auch über eine Moschee und eine Schule verfügt, wohnten damals Hunderte von Familien in Höhlen. Mitte des letzten Jahrhunderts wanderten die Jungen nach Tunis und bis nach Europa aus. Die wenigen Familien, die hier noch unterirdisch am Rande der Zivilisation ausharren, leben allerdings inzwischen nicht mehr so einsiedlerisch, auch ihr Misstrauen gegenüber der Außenwelt ist gesunken. Heutzutage eröffnen sich den Höhlenbewohnern neue Möglichkeiten der Zukunftssicherung: Zunehmend werden freundlich gesonnene Touristen an den stabilen Türen aus Palmholz willkommen geheißen.

À flanc de montagne, le *ksour* (village fortifié) domine les plaines caillouteuses du grand Sud tunisien. Telle des ruches géantes, des greniers fortifiés (*ghorfas*, en langue berbère) sont un entrelacs de pièces sur plusieurs étages accessibles de l'extérieur par des escaliers.

Depuis le Moyen-Âge, on se protège ici d'un monde extérieur hostile. L'époque a longtemps été aux razzias. Menacées par la guerre, les tribus n'avaient pas d'autre choix que de protéger leurs produits de première nécessité. Une des plus grandes curiosités architecturales d'Afrique du Nord est ainsi née de ce souci permanent de sécurité. Avec sa mosquée et son école, Matmata a longtemps été un vrai village troglodyte où vivaient une centaine de familles. Au milieu du siècle dernier, la jeunesse s'est exilée à Tunis et jusqu'en Europe. Aujourd'hui, quelques familles s'obstinent encore à vivre à l'écart du monde moderne dans des cavernes. Mais elles ne sont plus seules et encore moins hostiles. Ainsi le village troglodyte s'invente un nouveau destin pour l'avenir de ses enfants: l'étranger, en la personne du touriste, peut franchir en ami les solides portes en bois de palmier.

❋ **FACING PAGE** At the foot of their fortified granaries, *ghorfas* in the Berber language, the men go about the ceremony of serving tea. **ABOVE** Considered impregnable, these arched cells overlook the mountains and withstand the heaviest rains. ❋ **LINKE SEITE** Vor den befestigten Speichern, die in der Berbersprache *ghorfas* genannt werden, zelebrieren die Männer die Teezeremonie. **OBEN** Die wabenförmigen Gewölbe, die jedem Angriff standhalten sollen, thronen über den Bergen und trotzen selbst sintflutartigen Regenfällen. ❋ **PAGE DE GAUCHE** Au pied des greniers fortifiés, *ghorfas* en langue berbère, les hommes procèdent à la cérémonie du thé. **CI-DESSUS** Jugées imprenables en cas d'attaque, les cellules voûtées dominent les montagnes et résistent aux pluies diluviennes.

※ **ABOVE** The troglodyte abodes of Matmata have always resisted attacks by hostile tribes. **PAGES 140–145** There is very little furniture in these homes: nature supplies nearly every need. The chair, brought from town, is no more than a ghostly extra. Van Gogh, where are you? ※ **OBEN** Die Behausungen der Höhlenbewohner von Matmata erwiesen sich für feindliche Stämme als uneinnehmbar. **SEITEN 140–145** In diesem Wohnumfeld gibt es nur wenige Möbel – die Natur sorgt für das Nötigste. Der aus der Stadt mitgebrachte Stuhl dient eigentlich nur als Zierde. Van Gogh, bist du auch da? ※ **CI-DESSUS** Les habitations troglodytes de Matmata ont toujours résisté aux tribus hostiles. **PAGES 140–145** Peu de meubles dans cet habitat – la nature pourvoit aux besoins. La chaise, apportée de la ville, n'est qu'un élément de décor pour fantômes. Van Gogh, est-tu là?

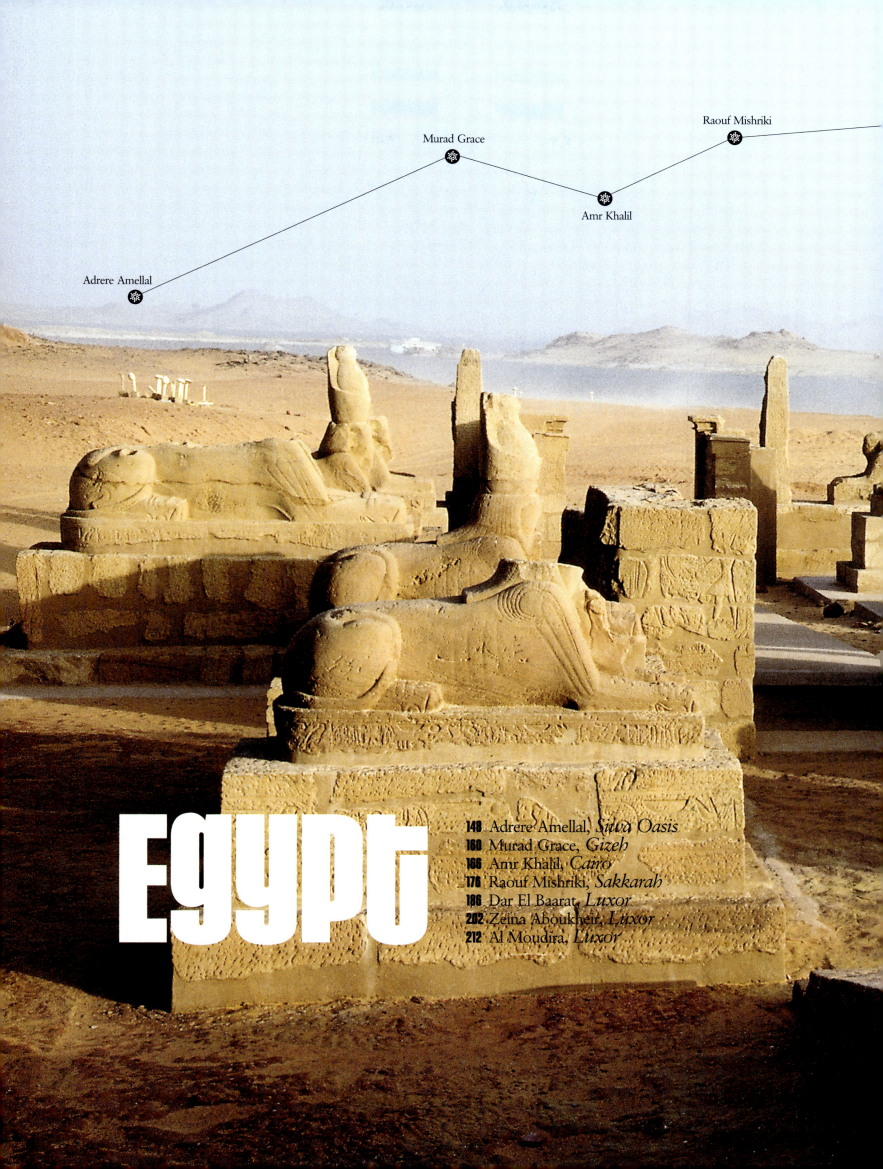

Adrere Amellal

Murad Grace

Raouf Mishriki

Amr Khalil

Egypt

Dar El Baarat

Al Moudira

Zeina Aboukheir

Adrere Amellal

Siwa Oasis

Herodotus called this place the "Island of the Blessed".
Today, it's home to a hotel of Biblical purity.

It's a day's drive over tracks from Cairo to Siwa, a Berber fortress standing against the waves of sand rolling in from the Libyan Desert. The oasis clings to a white mountain, moored to the silvery bank of a broad salt lake.

It has all the beauty of the Berber village it used to be; palm fronds clothe its roofs and new *pisé* covers its walls, now that the original Berber order has returned. The owner, Mounir Neamatalla, has made his dream come true – he has created an ecological village, the first in Egypt. His hotel was built without plans but following ancestral intuition, nestling harmoniously in a hollow of the nearby palm grove. Its eight buildings contain 34 bedrooms without telephone or electricity. With its terraces, high walls, narrow alleys and vegetable garden, the site has real authenticity, not to mention organically-grown food and the option of olive oil massages and incense-scented steam baths. There is even a meditation room.

Von Kairo muss man einen ganzen Tag auf den Pisten einplanen. Dann taucht Siwa auf, eine Berberfestung vor den Sandwogen der Lybischen Wüste. Dicht an den hohen Sanddünen und am silbernen Ufer eines riesigen Salzsees gelegen, präsentiert sich die Oase in der ganzen Pracht eines alten Berberdorfes.

Bei den auf traditionelle Art gebauten Häusern bestehen die Dächer aus Palmblättern und die Mauern aus Lehm. Der Eigentümer der Anlage, Mounir Neamatalla, verwirklicht hier seinen Lebenstraum: das erste Öko-Dorf Ägyptens. Das Hotel, das nicht auf dem Reißbrett sondern nach Art der Vorfahren entworfen wurde, liegt harmonisch in einer Senke neben einem Palmenhain. 34 Zimmer ohne Telefon und Elektrizität sind auf acht Gebäude verteilt. Mit den Terrassen, den hohen Mauern, engen Gassen und dem Gemüsegarten wirkt die Anlage wie ein Dorf aus vergangenen Zeiten. Die Gäste werden mit Biokost versorgt. Im Hammam werden Massagen mit Olivenöl und Aroma-Dampfbäder angeboten. Auch ein Meditationsraum ist vorhanden, in dem man erfährt, dass bereits Alexander der Große in Siwa war. Er wollte das Orakel befragen, ob er wirklich Zeus' Sohn sei.

Du Caire, il faut emprunter les pistes pendant une journée. Alors Siwa se devine, forteresse berbère où les vagues de sable du désert libyque viennent suspendre leur course. Accrochée à la montagne blanche, amarrée au rivage argenté d'un vaste lac salé, l'oasis dévoile la beauté d'un ancien village berbère.

Dans l'ordre retrouvé des habitations traditionnelles, les palmes habillent les toits, le pisé couvre les murs. Le propriétaire des lieux, Mounir Neamatalla, réalise ici son rêve: la naissance d'un village écolo, le premier d'Égypte. L'hôtel, bâti sans plans mais avec l'intuition ancestrale, est lové harmonieusement au creux de la palmeraie voisine. Ses huit bâtiments abritent 34 chambres sans téléphone ni électricité. Avec ses terrasses, ses hauts murs, ses ruelles étroites et son potager, le site a le charme d'un village d'antan. Le voyageur n'a plus qu'à découvrir les aliments bio. Au hammam, il apprécie les massages à l'huile d'olive et les bains de vapeur à l'encens. Il ne peut manquer la salle de méditation. On y apprend qu'Alexandre le Grand s'était rendu à Siwa pour consulter l'oracle et savoir s'il était bien le fils de Zeus.

✳ **ABOVE** The olive-wood furniture was made by Siwa craftsmen. The ochre stones in the walls alternate with partitions in *kershef*, a rough mixture of lake salt and clay from nearby. **FACING PAGE BELOW LEFT** Delicious bread is made in this oven, using traditional techniques. ✳ **OBEN** Handwerker aus Siwa stellen diese Möbel aus Olivenholz her. Die ockergelben Mauersteine kontrastieren mit den Zwischenwänden aus *kershef*, einem Gemisch aus dem Salz des Sees und Lehm aus der Nachbarschaft. **RECHTE SEITE UNTEN LINKS** Das köstliche Brot wird nach traditionellen Rezepten gebacken. ✳ **CI-DESSUS** Le mobilier en bois d'olivier est réalisé par les artisans de Siwa. Les pierres ocre des murs alternent avec des cloisons en *kershef*, un enduit rugueux, mélange de sel provenant du lac et des terres argileuses voisines. **PAGE DE DROITE EN BAS À GAUCHE** Un pain succulent est fabriqué dans le four selon les techniques traditionnelles.

❊ **ABOVE** The traditional furniture in the bedrooms was all made by the craftsmen of the oasis. The walls are made of yellow sand and clay. **FACING PAGE** At dusk, Siwa is magnified by the soothing light of paraffin lamps. ❊ **OBEN** Die althergebrachte Einrichtung der Zimmer wird ausschließlich von den Handwerkern der Oase hergestellt. Die Mauern bestehen aus hellgelbem Sand und Lehm. **RECHTE SEITE** Öllampen tauchen die Oase bei Sonnenuntergang zusätzlich in ein warmes Licht. ❊ **CI-DESSUS** Le mobilier traditionnel des chambres est entièrement conçu par les artisans de l'oasis. Les murs sont faits de sable blond et d'argile. **PAGE DE DROITE** Au crépuscule, Siwa est magnifiée par la lueur apaisante des lampes à pétrole.

✳ **ABOVE AND FACING PAGE** The bathrooms have running water, but remain faithful to tradition with this system of clothes-hangers made of wood and string. ✳ **OBEN UND LINKE SEITE** In den Badezimmern gibt es zwar fließendes Wasser, ansonsten sind sie jedoch der Tradition getreu eingerichtet, wie dieser Kleiderständer aus Holz und Schnüren veranschaulicht. ✳ **CI-DESSUS ET PAGE DE GAUCHE** Les salles de bains disposent de l'eau courante, mais restent fidèles aux anciennes traditions avec ce système de porte-vêtement à base de bois et de cordelettes.

MUraD GraCE

GiZEH

When functionalism meets the best local traditions,
the result is a shadow play of different epochs.

The acclaimed architect Hassan Fathy has been working for decades to accomplish the intellectual rehabilitation of his country's architectural traditions.

In his determination to find an oriental vocabulary for functionalism, he is convinced that his entire nation possesses a genius for architecture. The house of Murad Grace and his wife, off the Sakkarah Road at the edge of Cairo, is an example of his theory. It is sited away from the din of the city among shady palm trees, with the pyramid of Gizeh well in sight. The spaces are simple and freely articulated for maximum interplay. The house is very compact, but its studied use of vaulting makes it seem larger than it is. With a blend of lime and chalk, shallow domes and windows overlooking a kidney-shaped pool, it stands in stark contrast to the opulent houses of old Cairo. And yet when you see the old stones and beautiful objects all around you, there's no room for doubt: this house belongs here, in the Egypt of the Pharaohs.

Der mit Auszeichnungen überhäufte Architekt Hassan Fathy setzt sich seit Jahrzehnten für die intellektuelle Ehrenrettung des architektonischen Erbes seines Heimatlandes ein.

Er fördert einen orientalisch geprägten Funktionalismus, weil er davon überzeugt ist, dass sein Volk grundsätzlich über architektonisches Genie verfügt. Ein gutes Beispiel dafür ist das Haus von Murad Grace und seiner Frau an der Sakkarah Road in einem Außenbezirk von Kairo. Abseits der unruhigen Metropole liegt es im Schatten der Palmen mit direktem Blick auf die Pyramiden von Gizeh. Obwohl das Haus kompakt ist, lassen die vielen Gewölbe es größer erscheinen. Die niedrigen Kuppeln aus einer Kalk-Kreide-Mischung, deren Fenster zum Swimmingpool (in Form einer Bohne) hinausgehen, stehen in starkem Kontrast zu den üblichen Behausungen in der Altstadt von Kairo. Doch wenn der Blick die Steine liebkost oder auf den schönen Objekten ruht, wird spürbar, wie sehr dieses in der Nähe der Pharaonen gelegene Haus in Ägypten verwurzelt ist.

Bardé de récompenses, l'architecte Hassan Fathy s'est engagé pendant des années dans la réhabilitation intellectuelle du patrimoine architectural de son pays.

Dans sa volonté de décliner un fonctionnalisme à l'orientale, il est convaincu que son peuple, tout entier, possède un génie architectural. À la périphérie du Caire, sur Sakkarah Road, la demeure de Murad Grace et sa femme a valeur d'exemple. Elle est située loin des turbulences de la ville, à l'abri des palmiers, avec les pyramides de Gizeh dans la ligne de mire. Les volumes sont simples, articulés selon des plans d'une grande liberté, qui tendent à l'interpénétration des espaces. La maison est très compacte, mais le recours aux voûtes a permis de décupler la sensation d'espace. Avec son mélange de chaux et de craie, ses dômes peu profonds et ses fenêtres donnant sur une piscine en forme de haricot, le contraste est sensible pour celui qui débarque des maisons du vieux Caire. Et pourtant, quand l'œil caresse les pierres, quand il se pose sur de beaux objets, le doute n'est plus permis la demeure est en terre d'Égypte, non loin des pharaons.

❋ **ABOVE** As converts to the functionalist theories of the architect Hassan Fathy, the owners have decorated their house with ancestral objects such as these pieces of Nile pottery. **FACING PAGE** Arches and cupolas around the broad patio. ❋ **OBEN** Die Besitzer ließen sich von den funktionalistischen Theorien Hassan Fathys überzeugen und statteten ihre Räume mit antiken Gegenständen aus wie diesen Tonwaren, die in der Umgebung des Nils häufig gebraucht werden. **RECHTE SEITE** Bögen und Kuppeln rund um den Patio. ❋ **CI-DESSUS** Convertis aux théories fonctionnalistes de l'architecte Hassan Fathy, les propriétaires ont habillé les lieux d'objets ancestraux telles ces poteries traditionnelles du Nil. **PAGE DE DROITE** Succession de voûtes et de coupoles autour d'un grand patio.

✳ **ABOVE** The serenity of the *moucharabiehs* contrasts with the dusty street adjoining. **FACING PAGE** The walls are daubed with *helba* juice, to preserve the colour of the stone. ✳ **OBEN** Die gelassene Ausstrahlung der *moucharabiehs* steht in starkem Kontrast zur angrenzenden staubigen Straße. **RECHTE SEITE** Die Mauern wurden mit Helbasaft eingepinselt, damit die ursprüngliche Farbe der Steine erhalten bleibt. ✳ **CI-DESSUS** La sérénité des moucharabiehs contraste avec la poussiéreuse rue voisine. **PAGE DE DROITE** Les murs sont badigeonnés de jus d'*helba*, afin de préserver la couleur originelle de la pierre.

AMR KHALIL

Cairo

A variety of elegant styles come together in this apartment, which is geared to friendship and intimacy.

Ever since Voltaire observed, "It's all very fine, but each of us must cultivate his own garden," wise men have known that to escape the "convulsions of anxiety or the lethargy of ennui," nothing is better than a world of one's own.

As a disciple of the philosopher Pangloss, Amr Khalil has created an extraordinary place of culture and meditation which every morning permits him to reorganize his existence. He moves among Cairo's *gratin* and he loves his city; in the natural course of things he entertains, true to the ethic of his father, who was a great collector. Amr Khalil's cultural world is one that blends a variety of times and places. He has Second Empire beds amid exuberant Ottoman décor and Venetian furniture. Every object has its own story. Everything is prominently displayed, which (according to a Japanese friend) "is a mark of Amr's trust in mankind." He sees his domestic creation as a living organism with an organic logic of its own; stripped as it is of wallpaper to show the ageless patina of nakedness, and arranged according to the sole constraints of night and day.

Seit Voltaire und seinem berühmten Satz »Sehr richtig, aber wir müssen unseren Garten bestellen« weiß jeder kluge Mensch, dass es nichts Besseres gibt als ein eigenes Universum, um »den Zuckungen der Unrast oder der Trägheit der Langeweile« würdig zu begegnen.

Amr Khalil, ein weiser Schüler des guten Philosophen Pangloss, hat deshalb einen außergewöhnlichen Platz für Kultur und Meditation geschaffen, wo er allmorgendlich sein Leben neu in die Hand nimmt. Hier empfängt der Mann, der sich in seiner Stadt, der Wiege der Menschheit, gut auskennt und mit ihren Berühmtheiten vertraut ist, Gott und die Welt. Die berühmten Sammlungen seines Vaters sind in einem nach ihm benannten Museum ausgestellt. Das Universum des Sohnes vermengt die Stile und befreit sich von den Zwängen der Geografie. Die Betten aus dem Zweiten Kaiserreich harmonisieren die osmanische Fülle, die wiederum von den venezianischen Möbeln erst richtig zur Geltung gebracht wird. Jeder Gegenstand, jedes Möbelstück hat eine Geschichte. Das Ganze ist sichtbar arrangiert, ein Zeichen für »Amrs Vertrauen in die Menschheit«, wie ein japanischer Freund des Hausherrn feststellte. Der Eigentümer selbst sieht in seiner Kreation einen lebendigen Organismus mit einer inneren Logik. Deshalb kommt er auch ohne Tapeten aus und erzielt doch eine alterslose Patina, die sich nur den Zwängen von Tag und Nacht unterordnet.

Depuis Voltaire et son inoubliable «cela est bien dit, mais il nous faut cultiver notre jardin», les esprits sages savent que pour échapper «aux convulsions de l'inquiétude ou la léthargie de l'ennui», rien ne vaut un univers bien à soi.

En disciple du bon philosophe Pangloss, Amr Khalil a ainsi créé un lieu extraordinaire de culture et de méditation qui, chaque matin, lui permet d'organiser sa vie. Familier des célébrités du Caire et bien dans sa ville, ce berceau du monde, il reçoit, en bon fils d'un père dont les fameuses collections sont exposées dans un musée éponyme. Son univers brasse les périodes et s'affranchit de la géographie. Les lits Second Empire s'harmonisent avec une exubérance ottomane, elle-même relevée de meubles vénitiens. Chaque objet, chaque meuble a son histoire. L'ensemble est disposé bien en vue, ce qui, selon un ami japonais «reflète la confiance d'Amr en l'humanité». Le propriétaire voit sa création comme un organisme vivant doté d'une logique organique, dépouillé de ses papiers peints pour le nu évocateur d'une patine sans âge, ordonné selon les contraintes liées au jour et à la nuit.

※ **PAGES 170–173** The salon shows a number of different styles and periods – note the collection of unusual paintings. **FACING PAGE** The guest room and its two Napoleon III beds, side by side. **ABOVE** The guest bathroom with its 19th century looking glass. ※ **SEITEN 170–173** Im Salon mischen sich verschiedene Stile und Epochen. Bemerkenswert ist die bunt zusammengewürfelte Sammlung von Gemälden. **LINKE SEITE** Das Gästezimmer mit den beiden Betten aus der Epoche Napoleon III. **OBEN** Das Gästebad mit einem Spiegel aus dem 19. Jahrhundert.
※ **PAGES 170–173** Le salon embrasse une variété de styles et de périodes où l'on remarque une collection de tableaux hétéroclite. **PAGE DE GAUCHE** La chambre d'amis et ses deux lits Napoléon III placés côte à côte. **CI-DESSUS** La salle de bains des invités avec son miroir 19e.

RAOUF MISHRIKI

SAKKARAH

The vast necropolis of Memphis has more to it than pyramids –
as this house with its olive groves attests.

At the foot of the Pyramid of Djoser stands a house surrounded by 15 acres of olive groves. It's a breathtaking spot, with the olive trees, which are drenched in sunshine for 300 days a year, forming a natural barrier against the dunes of the Sahara.

Like the pharaohs who lived here before him, Raouf Mishriki venerates this delicate ecosystem. On his property, known as the Horus Estate, he built a house ten years ago whose absolute priority was harmony with its surroundings. Almost entirely composed of elements dating from the turn of the 19th century, it was modelled on a family property built a hundred years ago just north of Luxor. The finest craftsmen in the area were called in to refresh the dominant Arab and Turkish style, and in his concern for total authenticity Raouf Mishriki studiously avoided modern chrome and tiles; the pool in which he refreshes himself is a sacred one, like the ones in the old temples. Mishriki is as happy with his objects as he is with his olives, whose fruit is harvested here in just the same way as it was in antiquity. For him, the symbolic strength of a living tree is worth more than any museum piece.

Das Haus am Fuß der Djoser-Pyramide ist von einer sechs Hektar umfassenden Olivenpflanzung umgeben. Die Lage ist atemberaubend schön: Die Olivenbäume, die jährlich 300 Tage Sonne bekommen, bilden einen natürlichen Wall gegen die orangefarbenen Dünen der Sahara.

Raouf Mishriki, der hier am gleichen Ort lebt wie früher die Pharaonen, begeistert sich stets von neuem für dieses empfindliche Öko-System. Als er auf seinem nach dem Gott Horus benannten Landgut vor gut zehn Jahren ein Haus errichtete, stand die Harmonie mit der unmittelbaren Umgebung im Vordergrund seiner Überlegungen. Dabei inspirierte ihn ein Familienbesitz, der vor hundert Jahren im Norden Luxors gebaut worden war. So besteht das neue Haus fast ausschließlich aus wieder verwerteten Elementen aus dem 19. Jahrhundert. Mishriki musste sich an die besten Handwerker Ägyptens wenden, um dem dominanten arabisch-osmanischen Stil neue Impulse zu geben. Im Sinne der Authentizität verzichtete er auf Chrom und moderne Fliesen. Gebadet wird deshalb in einem heiligen Becken wie in den alten Tempeln. Der Hausherr schwärmt nicht nur von seinem Gut allgemein, sondern im Einzelnen von den Holzvertäfelungen, den Objekten und nicht zuletzt von den Olivenbäumen, deren Früchte auf althergebrachte Weise geerntet werden. In seiner symbolischen Aussagekraft ist ihm ein Baum mindestens ebenso viel wert wie ein Museumsstück.

Au pied de la pyramide de Djoser, la maison se dresse au milieu d'une oliveraie de six hectares. La beauté du site coupe le souffle. Baignés de soleil 300 jours par an, les oliviers forment un rempart naturel aux dunes orangées du Sahara.

À l'enseigne des pharaons, Raouf Mishriki vénère cette nature à l'écosystème si délicat. Sur son domaine dit d'Horus, il a édifié il y a une dizaine d'années une maison dont la priorité reste l'harmonie avec son environnement immédiat. Presque entièrement composée d'éléments de récupération datés du tournant du 19e siècle, elle s'inspire d'une propriété familiale édifiée il y a un siècle au nord de Louxor. Il a fallu recourir aux meilleurs artisans du pays pour rafraîchir le style arabo-turc dominant. Dans un souci d'authenticité, Raouf Mishriki a évité le piège des chromes et carreaux modernes. C'est donc dans un bassin sacré, à l'image de ceux des temples, que l'on se rafraîchit. Épris de son domaine, le propriétaire vénère tout autant ses boiseries et ses objets que ses oliviers dont les fruits sont récoltés comme dans l'Antiquité. Car ici, la valeur d'un arbre, dans sa force symbolique, vaut bien celle d'une pièce de musée.

Dar El Baarat Luxor

A stone's throw from the Valley of the Queens,
this fortress hides its whimsy under vaults and domes.

In the end, the house took root on the left bank of the Nile, where the dead are – which is anything but a bad augury in Egypt since according to tradition the dead sustain the living. It was something of a feat to get it built at all.

Chronic shortage of building materials, disputes with neighbours, sandstorms – Christian Louboutin, Parisian shoemaker and darling of the jet set, has survived them all. With its corner tower, its cupolas and its *pisé* walls, the casbah (which in this case really means citadel) is situated near the ruins of a village and a Coptic monastery. A disciple of Hassan Fathy, Egypt's most eminent architect (see the previous pages on the house of Murad Grace), Olivier Sednaoui conceived it in the oldest and noblest material known to man: mother earth. Its interior breathes the fantasy which has made Louboutin so famous as a maker of beautiful shoes. As soon as the gates open, you see the whole thing around you from the courtyard and its outside fireplace. Five bedrooms and two large living rooms share a succession of raised arches and domes. The colours are simple, the furniture stately, the site matchless.

Endlich steht dieses Haus am linken Nilufer, am Ufer der Toten – kein schlechtes Omen, nicht in Ägypten, wo die Toten traditionell die Lebenden nähren. Der Stoßseufzer »endlich« bezieht sich darauf, dass der Bau dieses Hauses eine große Leistung war.

Materialmangel, Streit mit den Nachbarn, häufige Sandstürme – Widrigkeiten, mit denen Christian Louboutin, der berühmte Pariser Schuhdesigner, der die Füße des Jetset kleidet, inzwischen bestens vertraut ist. Die Kasbah (im Sinne von Zitadelle) steht mit ihrem Eckturm, den Kuppeln und Lehmmauern nahe bei den Ruinen eines alten Dorfes und eines koptischen Klosters. Olivier Sednaoui, ein Schüler Hassan Fathys, des bekanntesten Architekten Ägyptens (siehe das Anwesen von Murad Grace), plante das Haus aus dem edelsten und ältesten Material der Welt: Mutter Erde. Innen spiegelt das Haus die Fantasie, die auch die Schuhkreationen des Designers bestimmt. Kaum ist man vom Hof mit seinem Außenkamin ins Haus getreten, erfasst der Blick die gesamte Raumordnung. Eine Flucht von Kuppeln und Gewölben verteilt sich auf fünf Zimmer und zwei große Salons. Wie eine Einladung zu biblischen Ursprüngen wirken die Schlichtheit des Tons und die Noblesse der Einrichtung auf uns.

Finalement, la maison s'est enracinée sur la rive gauche du Nil, celle des morts, ce qui n'est nullement mauvais signe en Égypte, puisque, selon la tradition, les défunts nourrissent les vivants. Le «finalement» s'impose car la bâtir a relevé de l'exploit.

La pénurie de matériaux, les querelles entre voisins, les fréquentes tempêtes de sable – Christian Louboutin, célèbre chausseur parisien qui habille les pieds de la jet-set, a tout connu. Avec sa tour d'angle, ses coupoles et ses murs en pisé, la casbah (au sens premier de citadelle) se trouve proche des ruines d'un ancien village et d'un monastère copte. En disciple d'Hassan Fathy, l'architecte égyptien le plus reconnu (voir pages précédentes la demeure de Murad Grace), Olivier Sednaoui l'a conçue dans le matériau le plus noble et le plus vieux du monde: notre mère la terre. À l'intérieur souffle la fantaisie qui préside aux créations du chausseur. Sitôt les portes ouvertes, de la cour où se dresse la cheminée extérieure, l'œil embrasse l'ensemble. Cinq chambres et deux grands salons se partagent une succession de voûtes et de coupoles échafaudées. Simplicité des tons sobres, noblesse du mobilier, nous sommes conviés à un retour aux origines bibliques.

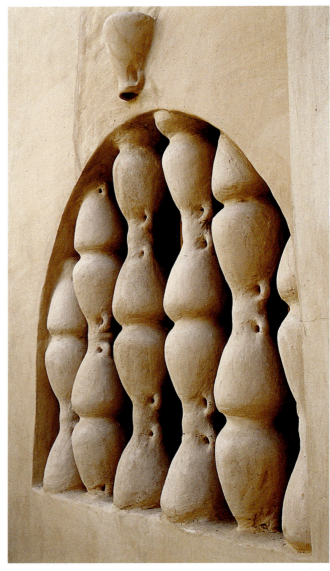

❋ **FACING PAGE** The building consists of a series of arches and domes constructed around a broad courtyard. **ABOVE** Unhappy with his *claustras*, Christian Louboutin replaced them with urns piled in front of the windows. ❋ **LINKE SEITE** Das Gebäude besteht aus einer Ansammlung von Gewölben und Kuppeln, die um den großen Hof herum gebaut wurden. **OBEN** Christian Louboutin gefielen die üblichen durchbrochenen Mauern (*claustras*) vor den Fenstern nicht, stattdessen wählte er Tonkruken. ❋ **PAGE DE GAUCHE** L'édifice est une succession de voûtes et de coupoles échafaudées autour de la grande cour. **CI-DESSUS** Mécontent de ses claustras, Christian Louboutin les a remplacés par des jarres empilées devant les fenêtres.

❋ **ABOVE** Bead-covered Nigerian chair and Cameroon table. **FACING PAGE** Sofa, chairs, giant copper chandeliers, *moucharabiehs*, Islamic inscriptions on marble, furniture inlaid with ivory and mother of pearl: Christian Louboutin seems to have stripped the souks of Cairo bare. ❋ **OBEN** Sessel aus Nigeria und Tisch aus Kamerun, mit Perlen besetzt. **RECHTE SEITE** Christian Louboutin hat die Souks in Kairo geplündert: Sofa, Stühle, gigantische Kupferlüster, *moucharabiehs*, islamische Inschriften in Marmor, Möbel mit Elfenbein- und Perlmuttintarsien. ❋ **CI-DESSUS** Fauteuil du Nigeria et table du Cameroun ornée de perles. **PAGE DE DROITE** Sofa, chaises, lustres géants en cuivre, moucharabiehs, inscriptions islamiques sur marbre, meubles incrustés d'ivoire et de nacre: Christian Louboutin a dévalisé les souks du Caire.

※ **PREVIOUS PAGES** In the dining room, the *zelligs* of the Moroccan-made table echo the rest of the décor, with its theme of North African art. The 1950's style chairs were picked up in Marrakesh, and the Baccarat chandelier came from Cairo. **LEFT** Christian Louboutin, the celebrated Parisian shoe designer. The lamp is in his honour. **BELOW** The ground floor guest bedroom. **FOLLOWING PAGE** On the upper floor, the owner's bedroom with its bedcover from Mali. ※ **VORHERGEHENDE DOPPELSEITE** Im Esszimmer symbolisiert der in Marokko aus *zelliges* gefertigte Tisch das von der maghrebinischen Kunst inspirierte Interieur. 1950er-Jahre-Stühle aus Marrakesch und ein Baccarat-Leuchter aus Kairo. **LINKS** Die Lampe ist Christian Louboutin, dem berühmten Pariser Schuhdesigner gewidmet. **UNTEN** Das Gästezimmer im Erdgeschoss. **FOLGENDE SEITE** Das Zimmer des Hausherrn im ersten Stock – die Tagesdecke stammt aus Mali. ※ **DOUBLE PAGE PRÉCÉDENTE** Dans la salle à manger, le jeu de zelliges de la table réalisée au Maroc fait écho à l'ensemble décoratif dédié à l'art maghrébin. Chaises de style années 1950 chinées à Marrakech. Chandelier Baccarat trouvé au Caire. **A GAUCHE** Christian Louboutin, le célèbre chausseur parisien. Lampe en hommage. **CI-DESSOUS** La chambre d'amis du rez-de-chaussée. **PAGE SUIVANTE** À l'étage, la chambre du propriétaire avec son dessus-de-lit provenant du Mali.

Zeina Aboukheir Luxor

A queen and her realm in the shadow of the Theban hills.

To lose, or to find oneself? Travel always leaves its addicts drained, at once stronger and more vulnerable, but always nearer to their own private truth.

After growing up in Lebanon and going all over the world, Zeina Aboukheir, a photographer and jewellery designer, came to rest at Luxor in a house adjoining the hotel she owns. Visiting its huge rooms is like reading Zeina's travel notebooks, and one delights in her furniture and antiques as if one were leafing through a record of her childhood. Take the salon and the dining room, where the history of the Near and Middle East is unfolded before one's eyes. Antique embroidered fabrics from Syria, of the type that were given to young married couples, cover the table and the cushions strewn on the banquettes. On a Caucasian kilim discovered in Jordan stand various items of *Retour d'Égypte* furniture dating from the 1930s. A painting from 1920 flirts with a ceiling lamp that bears the Ottoman insignia. On the walls, the frescoes by Mario Dahabi are a blend of eastern motifs and arabesques. On the floor, the cement tiles attest to the sheer willpower that went into the building of this place – for Zeina Aboukheir found some old moulds and engraved their original motifs herself. A true lover of Egypt, *la patronne* (as she is known to her workers) has set out to make the desert burst into flower. It may be that they have found a new queen in Luxor.

Die einen verlieren sich, die anderen finden sich – Reisende erleben sich stets ein wenig entrückt, mal stärker und mal schwächer, jedenfalls kommen sie ihrer eigenen Wahrheit näher.

Die Fotografin und Schmuckdesignerin Zeina Aboukheir wuchs im Libanon auf. Nachdem sie die Welt kennen gelernt hatte, blieb sie in Luxor – neben ihrem damaligen Hotel liegt heute ihr Haus. Wenn man durch die großen Räume schreitet, ist es, als lese man die Reisetagebücher der Künstlerin. Wer sich für ihre Möbel und die Antiquitäten begeistert, scheint in ihren Kindheitserinnerungen zu blättern. Nehmen wir zum Beispiel das Esszimmer: Vor unseren Augen präsentiert sich die Geschichte des Nahen und Mittleren Orients. Alte bestickte Stoffe aus Syrien, die früher jung verheirateten Paaren mitgegeben wurden, liegen auf dem Tisch und den Bankpolstern. Auf einem kaukasischen Kelim, den sie in Jordanien aufgetrieben hat, stehen Möbel im ägyptisierenden Stil der 1930er Jahre. Ein Gemälde von 1920 flirtet mit einer Deckenleuchte mit osmanischen Wappen. In den Fresken der Wände hat der Maler Mario Dahabi Wölbungen und Muster miteinander verwoben. Die Zementfliesen am Boden zeugen von der Hartnäckigkeit, die beim Bau dieses Hauses an den Tag gelegt wurde. Zeina Aboukheir besorgte sich alte Gussformen und ließ die Originalmuster eingravieren. Die »Herrin«, wie sie von den Bauarbeitern genannt wird, liebt Ägypten und würde am liebsten die Wüste begrünen. Ist sie die neue Königin?

Se perdre, ou se trouver – le voyage laisse toujours ses disciples un peu dépouillés, plus forts et plus faibles à la fois, mais toujours plus près de leur vérité.

Après avoir grandi au Liban et parcouru le monde, Zeina Aboukheir, photographe et dessinatrice de bijoux, a stoppé sa course à Louxor, dans cette maison qui jouxte son hôtel. On y découvre les vastes pièces comme on lirait ses carnets de voyage. On s'enthousiasme pour ses meubles et ses antiquités comme on feuilletterait ses souvenirs d'enfance. Prenez le salon et la salle à manger: l'histoire du Proche-Orient et du Moyen-Orient défile sous les yeux. De vieux tissus syriens brodés que l'on offrait aux jeunes mariés recouvrent la table et les coussins des banquettes. Sur un kilim caucasien découvert en Jordanie, des meubles «retour d'Égypte» des années 1930. Un tableau de 1920 flirte avec un plafonnier aux armes ottomanes. Au mur, les fresques peintent par Mario Dahabi mêlent courbes et motifs. Sur le sol, des carreaux de ciment témoignent de l'obstination déployée pour édifier les lieux. Zeina Aboukheir s'est procuré d'anciens moules et a fait graver les motifs originaux. Amoureuse de l'Égypte, «la patronne», selon les ouvriers du chantier, voulait fleurir le désert. Ont-ils trouvé une nouvelle reine ?

❋ **FOLLOWING PAGES** The salon, with its 1930s *Retour d'Égypte* furniture, mocks frontiers with its wooden *sourra* (ceiling), its chandelier with Ottoman insignia, and its carpet from the Caucasus. **PAGES 210–211** In the dining room, around an Art Deco table found in the flea market at Alexandria, the room is decorated with 19th century Damascus panels, a piece of Austrian-Italian furniture and an authentic Ottoman chandelier. ❋ **FOLGENDE DOPPELSEITE** Im Salon, der mit ägyptisierenden Möbeln aus den 1930er Jahren eingerichtet wurde, werden geografische Grenzen ignoriert, wie ein *sourra* (eine Deckenleuchte) aus Holz, ein Kronleuchter mit osmanischen Wappen und ein kaukasischer Kelim bezeugen. **SEITEN 210–211** Im Esszimmer, rund um den Art-déco-Tisch vom Flohmarkt in Alexandria, eine Tischlerarbeit aus altem Holz aus Damaskus (19. Jahrhundert), ein italienisch-österreichisches Möbelstück sowie an der Decke ein echter osmanischer Kronleuchter. ❋ **DOUBLE PAGE SUIVANTE** Le salon, autour d'un mobilier «retour d'Égypte» des années 1930, ignore les frontières avec sa *sourra* (plafonnier) en bois, son lustre aux armes ottomanes et son kilim caucasien. **PAGES 210–211** Dans la salle à manger, autour de la table Art Déco trouvée aux Puces d'Alexandrie, une pièce en vieux bois de Damas (19ᵉ siècle), un meuble italo-autrichien et, au plafond, un lustre ottoman authentique.

AL MOUDiRa
Luxor

On the shores of eternity, an oasis of peace in the grand tradition of Arabian palaces.

Zeina Aboukheir has realised a childhood dream with her hotel, an intricate complex of domes, columns, awnings and arabesques.

It stands on the West Bank of Luxor, at Thebes, birthplace of Hercules – and it is a wondrous blend of pleasure and refinement. With the architect Olivier Sednaoui (see also the house of Christian Louboutin) Zeina Aboukheir personally directed a building site of 150 labourers and craftsmen. There are hundred-year-old wood carvings brought here from grand ruined houses, along with ceramics, wrought iron and marquetry. The walls, painted in natural pigments, cover the entire range of ochres, red and blues formerly used for Egyptian houses and temples. Fountains add their music and their touch of freshness to the shaded calm of the pavilions. A short distance from the building, an enormous swimming pool with colonnades and fountains merges with the vegetation; and all around is a 20-acre garden burgeoning with lemon trees, mandarin orange trees, mangoes and goyabas. The brick alleys running through it are edged with palms, hibiscus and eucalyptus. This, unquestionably, is the best place hereabouts from which to view the sunset.

Zeina Aboukheir hat sich durch dieses Hotel mit all seinen Kuppeln, Bögen, Säulen, Vordächern und Arabesken einen Jugendtraum erfüllt.

Am Westufer von Luxor, in Theben, wo Herkules das Licht der Welt erblickte, gehen seitdem Freude und Raffinesse eine glückliche Verbindung ein. Das war nicht immer so! Gemeinsam mit dem Architekten Olivier Sednaoui (siehe das Haus von Christian Louboutin) leitete Zeina Aboukheir drei Jahre lang eine Baustelle mit 150 Arbeitern und Handwerkern. Die allgegenwärtigen Holzschnitzereien, die aus verfallenen Villen stammen, verbinden sich mit der Keramik, dem Schmiedeeisen und den Intarsienarbeiten. Die mit natürlichen Pigmenten gefärbten Mauern präsentieren die gesamte Palette von Ocker über Rot zu Blau, die bereits die alten Ägypter für ihre Häuser und Tempel benutzten. Brunnen unterstreichen plätschernd und erfrischend die schattige Ruhe der Pavillons. Ein wenig abseits fügt sich das große Becken des Pools, umgeben von Säulen und einem Brunnen, in die prächtige Landschaft. Im Hotelgarten wachsen Zitronen- und Mandarinenbäume, Orangen-, Mango- und Guajavabäume. Dazu kommen Palmen, Hibiskus in leuchtenden Farben sowie Eukalyptus, die den Rand der Ziegelpfade zieren. Von hier aus hat man einen wunderbaren Blick auf den Sonnenuntergang.

C'est un rêve de jeunesse que réalise Zeina Aboukheir en recevant dans son hôtel, cet entrelacs de coupoles, d'arcs, de colonnes, d'auvents et d'arabesques.

Sur la rive ouest de Louxor, à Thèbes, là où Hercule vit le jour, plaisir et raffinement se conjuguent désormais. C'est nouveau. Qu'on se le dise! Avec l'architecte Olivier Sednaoui (voir également la maison de Christian Louboutin), Zeina Aboukheir a dirigé pendant trois ans un chantier de 150 artisans et ouvriers. Partout, des bois sculptés centenaires, provenant de riches demeures délabrées, jouent à cache-cache avec la céramique, le fer forgé et la marqueterie. Les murs colorés de pigments naturels conjuguent la palette d'ocres, de rouges et de bleus autrefois utilisée pour les habitations et les temples égyptiens. Des fontaines ajoutent leur musique et leur note de fraîcheur au calme ombragé des pavillons. À l'écart, le vaste bassin de la piscine, avec ses colonnades et ses fontaines, s'intègre au décor végétal. Autour, le jardin de huit hectares mélange citronniers, mandariniers, orangers, manguiers et goyaviers. Palmiers, flamboyants, hibiscus et eucalyptus bordent les allées de brique. C'est d'ici que l'on apprécie le coucher du soleil.

❋ **ABOVE AND FACING PAGE** Corbels, cornices and high ceilings lend the hotel its own air of serene majesty. In the entrance courtyard, a *moucharabieh* filters the light. The carved wood, some of it a century old, was salvaged from abandoned houses. The marquetry was copied from Mameluke originals (the Mamelukes reigned in Egypt from 1250 to 1517). ❋ **OBEN UND RECHTE SEITE** Die Auskragungen, Kranzgesimse und hohen Decken verleihen dem Hotel eine heitere Großartigkeit. Im Eingangshof filtert ein *moucharabieh* das Licht. Die an manchen Stellen hundert Jahre alten Holzschnitzereien stammen aus verlassenen Villen. Die Intarsienarbeiten wurden nach mameluckischem Vorbild angefertigt (Die Mamelucken herrschten von 1250 bis 1517 in Ägypten). ❋ **CI-DESSUS ET PAGE DE DROITE** Les encorbellements, corniches et hauts plafonds donnent à l'hôtel une majesté sereine. Dans la cour d'entrée, un moucharabieh filtre la lumière. Le bois sculpté, parfois centenaire, a été récupéré dans des maisons abandonnées. La marqueterie est réalisée selon le travail mamelouk (dynastie qui régna de 1250 à 1517 en Égypte).

❊ **FACING PAGE** In the dining room, chandeliers of glass and copper, with wrought iron tables from all over Egypt. **BELOW** An immense Syrian frame, with 18th century Ottoman-Italian motifs, overlooks the bar with its sofas and Karabakh kilim. ❊ **LINKE SEITE** Im Esszimmer hängen Kristall- und Kupferlüster über schmiedeeisernen Tischen. **UNTEN** Ein riesiger syrischer Rahmen mit italo-osmanischen Mustern aus dem 18. Jahrhundert hängt über der sofabestückten Bar. Kelim aus Karabach. ❊ **PAGE DE GAUCHE** Dans la salle à manger, des lustres en verre ou cuivre, ainsi que des tables en fer forgé choisis aux quatre coins d'Égypte. **CI-DESSOUS** Un immense cadre syrien, aux motifs italo-ottomans du 18e siècle, domine le bar avec ses sofas et son kilim du Karabakh.

❋ **PRECEDING DOUBLE PAGE, BELOW AND FACING PAGE** In the bedrooms are king-size beds, in the Ottoman style. The frescoes were painted by the Lebanese artist Mario Dahabi, assisted by "Tayeb Picasso", a craftsman from Gurna. The *suzani* (embroidered fabric) comes from Jordan. ❋ **VORHERGEHENDE DOPPELSEITE, UNTEN UND RECHTE SEITE** In den Zimmern stehen Kingsize-Betten nach osmanischem Vorbild. Mario Dahabi malte die Fresken mit Hilfe von »Tayeb Picasso«, einem Handwerker aus Gurna. Der *suzani* (bestickter Stoff) stammt aus Jordanien. ❋ **DOUBLE PAGE PRÉCÉDENTE, CI-DESSOUS ET PAGE DE DROITE** Dans les chambres, des lits de taille «royale», fabriqués à la manière ottomane. Les fresques ont été peintes par l'artiste libanais Mario Dahabi aidé de «Tayeb Picasso», un artisan de Gurna. Le *suzani* (tissu brodé) provient de Jordanie.

Anna Trzebinski

Kitengela Glass

Alan Donovan

The Giraffe Manor

Sirocco House

Dodo's Tower

Hippo Point

Armando Tanzini

Katharina Schmezer
& Hermann Stucki

Yago Casado

kenya

anna Trzebinski
Nairobi

At the edge of a reserve, this warm interior
offers a happy blend of cosiness and wild nature.

Only 25 minutes from Nairobi, this cottage faced in pale wood is a combination of scattered influences from the African and European continents.

Yes, this is Kenya, but there is a certain English charm about this spot; Russian, too, to judge by the bare and massive tree trunks nearby, which make you think of dachas and Anna Karenina; and Indian, when you see the delicate Indian fabrics inside. Anna Trzebinski, the owner, will tell you that amid the immense freedom of the land she lives in, these odd collisions generate a sense of eternity. Her husband Tonio, born in Africa of Polish parents, spent much of his life on safari (the Swahili word means "journey") in the great plains of East Africa. The contemporary furniture, which he created for himself, was all cut straight from tree trunks to evoke the idea of nature. Mission accomplished. From the terrace overlooking the forest, giraffes can often be seen feeding on the nearby foliage. Here we are close to the bush, and the sound of rain pattering on the corrugated iron roof is balm to the soul.

Das Cottage aus hellem Holz, von Nairobi mit dem Auto in nur 25 Minuten zu erreichen, vereint Einflüsse aus Europa und Afrika. Stimmt, wir sind in Kenia. Aber ist es nicht stellenweise reizend englisch?

Und diese mächtigen Säulen aus nackten Baumstämmen, beschwören sie nicht eine Datscha, aus der jeden Moment Anna Karenina und die Ihren hervorkommen könnten? Anna Trzebinski selbst glaubt, dass die ungeheure Freiheit des Ortes, die klaren Gegensätze, ein Gefühl von Ewigkeit schüren. Ihr Mann Tonio, ein gebürtiger Afrikaner polnischer Abstammung, war schon oft auf Safari (das Kisuaheliwort bedeutet »Reise«) in den weiten Ebenen Ostafrikas. Die modernen Möbel, die er selbst entworfen hat, werden direkt aus Baumstämmen geschreinert, um so natürlich wie möglich zu wirken. Das ist ihm gelungen. Von den Terrassen, die den Blick in den Wald freigeben, kann man Giraffen beobachten, die sich von den Blättern der umstehenden Bäume ernähren. Der Busch ist nah; hier hat selbst der Regen eine angenehme Melodie. Sein Prasseln auf dem Wellblechdach beruhigt auch nervöse Gemüter.

À tout juste 25 minutes de Nairobi, le cottage paré de bois blond rassemble des influences éparses entre les continents africain et européen. Oui, nous sommes au Kenya. Mais ici et là ne flotte-il pas un charme à l'anglaise?

Et ces puissantes colonnes de troncs d'arbre nus, n'évoquent-elles pas une datcha d'où surgiraient Anna Karénine et les siens? Et que dire de ces délicates étoffes indiennes? Interrogez Anna Trzebinski, elle vous dira que l'immense liberté des lieux, cette collision limpide, génère un sentiment d'éternité. Enfant d'Afrique d'origine polonaise, son mari Tonio a passé une bonne partie de sa vie en safari (mot swahili signifiant «voyage») dans les grandes plaines de l'Afrique orientale. Les meubles contemporains qu'il a lui-même créés ont été taillés dans des troncs d'arbre afin d'évoquer la nature. Mission accomplie. Des terrasses qui surplombent la forêt, il n'est pas rare d'observer les girafes qui se nourrissent aux branches voisines. On est à proximité de la brousse. La pluie est mélodieuse. Son cliquetis sur le toit en tôle ondulée calme même les plus agités.

✳ **FACING PAGE** Built on two levels, the house has a broad ground floor living room, bedrooms on the first floor and an attic at the top. **ABOVE** The living room opens onto the terrace. The flooring is made of mahogany. ✳ **LINKE SEITE** Das zweigeschossige Haus besteht aus einem großen Wohnzimmer im Erdgeschoss, einigen Zimmern auf der ersten Etage und einem Speicher unterm Dach. **OBEN** Der Salon geht auf die Terrasse hinaus. Das Parkett ist aus Mahagoni. ✳ **PAGE DE GAUCHE** Bâtie sur deux niveaux, la maison comporte un large living au rez-de-chaussée, des chambres à l'étage et un grenier au sommet. **CI-DESSOUS** Le salon s'ouvre sur la terrasse. Le parquet est en acajou.

✳ **ABOVE** The living room furniture was all made by Tonio Trzebinski from tree trunks. On the walls are drawings and paintings by him. Around the chimney with its rough beams, three sofas with slipcovers. **FACING PAGE** In the dining room, a massive tabletop resting on tree trunks. ✳ **OBEN** Der Salon mit den von Tonio Trzebinski selbst gefertigten Möbeln. An den Wänden hängen Zeichnungen und Bilder von ihm. Um den mit rohen Balken gerahmten Kamin stehen drei mit Hussen bezogene Sofas. **RECHTE SEITE** Der Tisch im Esszimmer besteht aus einer riesigen Platte, die auf vier Baumstämmen ruht. ✳ **CI-DESSUS** Le salon et ses meubles fabriqués à même l'arbre par Tonio Trzebinski. Aux murs, ses dessins et tableaux. Autour de la cheminée garnie de poutres brutes, trois sofas houssés. **PAGE DE DROITE** La table de la salle à manger, un énorme plateau posé sur quatre troncs.

❋ **FACING PAGE AND LEFT** The low table cut from tree trunks serves as a glass cabinet containing Trzebinski's safari souvenirs. **BELOW** On the bookshelves in the living room, a collection of local headrests – used by men and women at night so their elaborate coiffures won't be spoiled. ❋ **LINKE SEITE UND LINKS** In den niedrigen aus Baumstämmen geschnittenen Vitrinen liegen Souvenirs von verschiedenen Safaris. **UNTEN** In der Bibliothek ist eine Sammlung von Kopfstützen verschiedener Stämme ausgestellt. Darauf legen die Frauen und Männer nachts den Nacken, damit die Frisur nicht leidet. ❋ **PAGE DE GAUCHE ET À GAUCHE** Les tables basses taillées dans des troncs d'arbre sont des vitrines qui abritent des souvenirs de safari. **CI-DESSOUS** Dans la bibliothèque du salon, une collection de repose-tête régionaux, la nuit les femmes et les hommes y appuient la nuque afin de ne pas abîmer leurs coiffures.

❋ **PREVIOUS PAGES** The bed, also cut from tree trunks, is protected by a mosquito net affixed to the ceiling with a series of curtain rods. The safari trunks picked up in Nairobi give the bedroom the air of a camp in the bush. **ABOVE** An ethno-chic touch in the bathroom, with these Indian silk curtains. **FACING PAGE** The wooden kitchen building stands apart from the house. Small openings all round the roof create a pool of light below. In the midst of all the African utensils stands a wooden Indian kitchen table. ❋ **VORHERGEHENDE DOPPELSEITE** Über dem aus Baumstämmen geschreinerten Bett hängt ein an mehreren Stangen befestigtes Moskitonetz. Die in Nairobi erstandenen Safarikoffer geben dem Raum den Anstrich eines Zeltlagers. **OBEN** Die Vorhänge aus indischer Seide verleihen dem Bad einen Hauch von Ethno-Chic. **RECHTE SEITE** Die in Holz eingerichtete Küche liegt neben dem Haus. Die kleinen Oberlichter rundherum sorgen für genügend Helligkeit. In dem Sammelsurium afrikanischer Küchenutensilien steht ein indischer Holztisch. ❋ **DOUBLE PAGE PRÉCÉDENTE** Le lit taillé dans des troncs d'arbres est surmonté d'une moustiquaire fixée au plafond par une série de tringles. Les malles de safari chinées à Nairobi font de la chambre un véritable campement. **CI-DESSOUS** Touche ethno-chic dans la salle de bains avec ces rideaux en soierie indienne. **PAGE DE DROITE** La cuisine en bois est indépendante de la maison. De petites ouvertures percées autour du toit créent un puits de lumière. Au milieu des ustensiles africains, une table indienne en bois.

Kitengela Glass

Nairobi

This family creates fantasies that might have been inspired by Antoni Gaudí or Niki de Saint-Phalle – out of glass, and against all expectations.

How on earth does the Kitengela factory survive, at the end of a rocky track that breaks up in the dry season and washes away in the wet? How do its glasses, vases, plates and carafes resist the onslaught of Africa's capricious outback?

Nani Croze has a ready answer: "We work among the animals, under the shade of bouganvilleas and acacias. The beauty of this place protects and inspires us." The visitor, already hypnotized by a broad palette of colours that includes cobalt blue and deep greens, discovers sculptures and wrought iron gates; even the workshops are multi-hued. In the "metal shop", Francis the blacksmith adds the final touches to a gigantic mirror destined for a Nairobi hotel. Farther on, like red mushrooms pushing out of the ground, are the bead and glass workshops, and beside these is a small shop in which the "village people" come to pick up supplies when the rhythm of their work allows. There's no shortage of work here: orders come in from all over the world. Seconded by her son Anselm and her daughter Katrineka, a specialist in jewellery made of blown glass, Nani Croze is part of a real working community. One wonders, how do the words *Sagrada Familia* translate into Masai?

Warum in aller Welt liegt die Fabrik Kitengela an einer steinigen Piste, die in der Trockenzeit voller Schlaglöcher ist und in der Regenzeit im Schlamm versinkt? Wie halten die Gläser, Vasen, Teller und Karaffen diese Schocktherapie der launischen afrikanischen Natur aus?

Darauf antwortet Nani Croze: »Wir arbeiten mitten unter den Tieren, im Schatten der Bougainvillea und Akazien. Die Schönheit des Ortes schützt und inspiriert uns ganz außerordentlich.« Der Besucher ist zunächst geradezu hypnotisiert von der Farbpalette, deren Schwerpunkt auf Kobaltblau und dunklen Grüntönen liegt. Dann entdeckt er die Skulpturen, die schmiedeeisernen Portale und als I-Tüpfelchen die bunten Ateliers. Im »Metal Shop« legt Francis, der Kunstschmied, letzte Hand an einen riesigen Spiegel, ein Auftragswerk des größten Hotels in Nairobi. Etwas entfernt liegen wie sprießende rote Pilze das Atelier, in dem mit Perlen und Glas gearbeitet wird, und der kleine Laden, in dem die »Dorfbewohner« ihren Bedarf decken – je nach Geschmack und Angebot. An Arbeit mangelt es nicht, aus der ganzen Welt gehen Aufträge ein. Nani Croze arbeitet gemeinsam mit ihrem Sohn Anselm und ihrer Tochter Katrineka, die sich auf Glasbläserei-Schmuck spezialisiert hat. Also, wie übersetzt man Sagrada Familia in die Sprache der Massai?

Par quel mystère la fabrique de Kitengela s'est-elle retrouvée au-delà d'une piste rocailleuse défoncée en saison sèche et submergée par les torrents en saison humide? Comment verres, vases, assiettes et carafes résistent-ils aux traitements de choc de la capricieuse nature africaine?

Réponse de Nani Croze: «Nous travaillons parmi les animaux, à l'ombre des bougainvilliers et des acacias. La beauté des lieux nous protège et nous donne une incroyable inspiration.» En visite, hypnotisé par une large palette de couleurs où dominent le bleu cobalt et les verts profonds, le voyageur découvre des sculptures, des portails en fer forgé ou, encore, des ateliers multicolores. Dans le «métal shop», Francis le ferronnier donne la dernière touche à un gigantesque miroir destiné au plus grand hôtel de Nairobi. Plus loin, tout droit sorti de terre comme les champignons rouges, l'atelier de perles et de verre, jouxte la mini-épicerie dans laquelle les «villageois» viennent s'approvisionner à leur guise, selon le rythme des créations du moment. Le labeur ne manque pas: les commandes viennent du monde entier. Secondée par son fils Anselm et par sa fille Katrineka, spécialiste des bijoux en verre soufflé, Nani Croze travaille en communauté. Au fait, comment traduit-on Sagrada Familia en langue Massaï?

※ **FACING PAGE** In the shower, bottle bottoms filter the light. **ABOVE** The family architect, the youngest son Lengai, designed the house of his sister Katrineka on the basis of a hut. ※ **LINKE SEITE** In der Dusche filtert eine Ansammlung von Flaschen das Licht. **OBEN** Der jüngste Sohn Lengai ist gleichzeitig der Architekt der Familie. Er hat das Haus seiner Schwester Katrineka in Form einer Hütte gestaltet. ※ **PAGE DE GAUCHE** Dans la douche, les culs de bouteille renversés filtrent la lumière. **CI-DESSUS** L'architecte de la famille, le fils cadet Lengai, a dessiné la maison de sa sœur Katrineka sur la base d'une hutte.

✳ **ABOVE** Nani Croze, who was born into a family of artists, learned to paint and sculpt in her childhood. In its forms and materials, her house is inspired by Masai tradition. ✳ **OBEN** Aus einer Künstlerfamilie stammend beschäftigte sich Nani Croze schon als Kind mit Malerei und Bildhauerei. Ihr Umfeld orientiert sich in den Formen und Materialien an den Traditionen der Massai. ✳ **CI-DESSUS** Née dans une famille d'artistes, Nani Croze a appris la peinture et la sculpture dès l'enfance. Dans ses formes comme dans ses matériaux, l'habitat est inspiré des traditions Massai.

※ **ABOVE** Christmas tree baubles, carafes, glasses, vases and lamps are on show in the shop, along with jewellery designed by Katrineka Croze. **FACING PAGE** The glass-blower at work. ※ **OBEN** Im Geschäft werden Weihnachtsbaumkugeln, Karaffen, Gläser, Vasen, Lampen und die von Katrineka Croze entworfenen Schmuckstücke ausgestellt. **RECHTE SEITE** Der Glasbläser bei der Arbeit. ※ **CI-DESSOUS** Boules de Noël, carafes, verres, vases, lampes, ainsi que les bijoux dessinés par Katrineka Croze sont exposés à la boutique. **PAGE DE DROITE** Le souffleur de verre à l'œuvre.

❈ **FOLLOWING PAGES** The sight of mosaics, sculpture and fantastically-shaped houses comes as a shock in the middle of the bush. In the garden stands a huge mosaic dragon. ❈ **FOLGENDE DOPPEL-SEITE** Der Anblick von Mosaiken, Skulpturen und Phantasie-Häusern erstaunt in der Savanne. Im Garten steht ein Drache aus Mosaiksteinen. ❈ **DOUBLE PAGE SUIVANTE** Voir des mosaïques, des sculptures et des maisons fantaisistes surprend dans la savane. Au centre du jardin, un immense dragon en mosaïque annonce la couleur.

ALAN DONOVAN
NairoBi

This American, who has lived in Kenya for 30 years,
is responsible for the famous African Heritage Collection.

Alan Donovan has found a mission of his own: a dedicated servant of the arts, he exports African craftwork all over the world.

In 1969, disillusioned with his US State Department job administering famine relief in the breakaway Nigerian region of Biafra, he quit government service, bought a VW bus in Paris, and went off to discover the rest of Africa. Years later he founded The African Heritage, a complex including pan-African galleries, gift shops, restaurants, craft centres and a festival which travels the world promoting African tourism and culture. The heart of Donovan's company beats in a house facing Mount Kilimanjaro. Built far out in the bush to his own design, and to plans by architect David Bristow, it responds to its owner's obsession with integrating traditional African art into a contemporary living space. Donovan's treasures, bought from a multitude of African countries, unite to form a concentrated gallery of the continent he loves; in all likelihood, he says, the house will become a museum after he is gone. May the Gods grant him many more years to show the world the wonders of Africa.

Alan Donovan hat seine Mission gefunden: Im Dienst der Künste exportiert er afrikanisches Kunsthandwerk in die ganze Welt.

Desillusioniert von seiner Arbeit, im Dienst des US-Außenministeriums Hungerhilfe für Kinder im separatistischen Biafra in Nigeria zu leisten, gab er 1969 seinen Job auf, kaufte in Paris einen VW-Bus und machte sich auf den Weg, das restliche Afrika zu entdecken. Viele Jahre später gründete er die African Heritage, ein komplexes Unternehmen aus panafrikanischen Gallerien, Geschenkboutiquen, Restaurants, Handwerksbetrieben und einem Festival zur Förderung der Kultur und des Tourismus in Afrika. Das Herz dieses Unternehmens schlägt in einem Haus in der Savanne – in Sichtweite des Kilimandscharo. Donavans Entwurf und die Pläne des Architekten David Bristow berücksichtigen die Besessenheit des Hausherrn und integrieren die traditionelle afrikanische Kunst in ein modernes Umfeld. Bunt zusammengewürfelte Schätze aus den unterschiedlichsten afrikanischen Ländern sind hier derart konzentriert versammelt, dass man das Haus mühelos in ein Museum verwandeln könnte, wenn der Besitzer einmal nicht mehr da wäre. Mögen die afrikanischen Gottheiten noch viele Jahre über Alan Donovan wachen, damit er auch weiterhin der Welt die Wunder Afrikas zeigen kann.

Alan Donovan s'est trouvé lui aussi une mission: au service des arts, il exporte dans le monde entier l'artisanat africain.

Déçu par son travail au Département d'État dans le service de l'Aide alimentaire pour les enfants du Biafra, région séparatiste du Nigeria, il démissionne en 1969, s'achète un minibus à Paris et part à la découverte de l'Afrique. Bien des années plus tard, il fonde African Heritage, une société complexe recouvrant des galeries panafricaines, des boutiques de souvenirs, des restaurants, des entreprises artisanales et un festival visant à promouvoir la culture et le tourisme africains. Le cœur de cette société bat dans une maison édifiée dans la savane, à portée de vue du Kilimandjaro. Le projet de Donavan et les plans de l'architecte David Bristow préservent l'obsession du maître des lieux: intégrer l'art traditionnel africain dans un espace contemporain. Des trésors hétéroclites glanés un peu partout évoquent un concentré d'Afrique, au point que la maison pourrait se transformer en musée à la disparition de son propriétaire. Puissent les divinités vernaculaires veiller encore longtemps sur Alan Donavan pour qu'il continue à nous montrer les merveilles de l'Afrique.

※ **ABOVE** The house has a glorious view across the Nairobi National Park to Kilimanjaro. **FOLLOWING PAGES** The swimming pool, built of Mazeras stone from the Kenyan Coast. The pool house has a roof made of *makuti* palm leaves. ※ **OBEN** Das Haus bietet einen großartigen Ausblick auf den Nairobi Nationalpark und den Kilimandscharo. **FOLGENDE DOPPELSEITE** Das Schwimmbad aus Mazeras-Steinen von der Küste Kenias. Das Dach des Pool House besteht aus *makuti* (Palmfasern). ※ **CI-DESSUS** La maison dispose d'une vue superbe sur le parc national de Nairobi et le Kilimandjaro. **DOUBLE PAGE SUIVANTE** La piscine, en pierre de Mazeras de la côte du Kenya. La *pool house* est surmontée d'un toit en fibres de *makuti*.

✴ **PREVIOUS PAGES** In the salon, the walls are painted with ethnic motifs and the beams encrusted with pebbles which create a mosaic effect. The floors are covered with woven palm mats. **FACING PAGE** A Moon Mask from Burkina Faso. ✴ **VORHERGEHENDE DOPPELSEITE** Ethnische Motive zieren die mit Pigment gestrichenen Mauern im Salon, während die Kieselintarsien auf den Balken wie Mosaike wirken. Geflochtene Palmmatten bedecken die Böden. **RECHTE SEITE** Mondmaske aus Burkina Faso. ✴ **DOUBLE PAGE PRÉCÉDENTE** Dans le salon, les murs sont peints de motifs ethniques et les poutres incrustées de cailloux dessinent une mosaïque. Sols recouverts de feuilles de palmier tressées. **PAGE DE DROITE** Masque-lune du Burkina Faso.

❊ **FACING PAGE** The four-poster bed is draped with Kuba ceremonial fabrics from the Congo. **BELOW** One of the bathrooms has its own garden, while the other has a tub set into stone from Masai Mara. ❊ **LINKE SEITE** Über dem Himmelbett liegen festliche Kuba-Stoffe aus dem Kongo. **UNTEN** Eines der Bäder hat eine Tür zu einem eigenen Garten, während das andere über eine Badewanne verfügt, die etwas erhöht in Orginalsteine aus dem Massai-Mara-Nationalpark eingelassen ist. ❊ **PAGE DE GAUCHE** Le lit à baldaquin est revêtu de tissus de cérémonie Kuba provenant du Congo. **CI-DESSOUS** Une des salles de bains est agrémentée d'un jardin extérieur, tandis que l'autre bénéficie d'une baignoire encastrée dans une estrade de pierre originaire du Massaï Mara.

THE Giraffe Manor
Nairobi

An archetypal British manor house –
and a charming reminder of the colonial past.

This Elizabethan house with neo-Gothic influences is worth the journey to East Africa all on its own. Fortified by the secular canons of good taste that are the preserve of Her Majesty's subjects, its owners have carefully maintained the country house atmosphere of their residence ever since 1932.

It has geometrical pediments, regulation brick masonry, a heavy front door, and plenty of noble materials and Gothic vaulting; indeed in every way it is a hymn to Britannia, despite being 4,500 feet above sea level. The giraffes are visibly appreciative. In the park, visitors may sit on a circular platform nine feet above the ground and proffer buckets of oats to these enormous creatures. It's a unique opportunity to observe their tongues – which are 18 inches long – as well as the sunset over the Rift Valley and the perfectly aligned tea and coffee plantations. Traces of some of the earliest human ancestors were found near this spot.

Schon dieses elisabethanische Haus mit neugotischen Zügen ist eine Reise wert. Die Eigentümer, die sich jenem Ideal des guten Geschmacks verpflichtet haben, das die Untertanen Ihrer Majestät geprägt hat, bemühen sich seit 1932, die »Landhaus«-Atmosphäre ihrer Villa zu erhalten.

Die geometrischen Frontgiebel, die traditionellen Ziegel britischer Häuser, die Eingangstür aus Massivholz, die Verbindung edler Baumaterialien, gotische Kreuzrippengewölbe – da scheint in 1500 Metern Höhe »Rule Britannia« zu erklingen, so patriotisch wirkt das Gebäude. Den Giraffen gefällt es offenbar. Im Park können die Touristen den großen Tieren von einer drei Meter hohen runden Plattform aus Eimer mit Getreide anbieten. Wo kann man schon wie hier ihre 45 Zentimeter lange Zunge aus nächster Nähe bewundern? In der Abenddämmerung geht die Sonne über dem Rifttal und den sorgsam angelegten Tee- und Kaffeeplantagen unter. In dieser Gegend wurden die Spuren von einigen der ältesten menschlichen Vorfahren gefunden.

Située au cœur de l'Afrique orientale, cette maison élisabéthaine aux influences néogothiques est, à elle seule, un but de voyage. Portés par l'idéal séculaire du bon goût que l'on prête aux sujets de Sa Majesté, ses propriétaires veillent depuis 1932 à préserver l'atmosphère «maison de campagne» de leur résidence.

Frontons aux lignes géométriques, briques traditionnelles des demeures britishs, porte d'entrée en bois massif, association de matériaux nobles, ogives gothiques, c'est un chant aux accents patriotiques très «Rule, Britannia» qui s'élève à cette altitude (nous sommes à plus de 1500 mètres). Les girafes, visiblement, apprécient. Dans le parc, depuis une plateforme circulaire située à trois mètres au-dessus du sol, le visiteur peut tendre à ces géantes des seaux pleins de céréales. Une chance unique d'observer de près leur langue longue de 45 centimètres! À la nuit tombée, le soleil se couche au-dessus de la vallée du Rift et des plantations de thé et de café soigneusement alignées. On a découvert ici les traces des plus anciens ancêtres des hommes.

✳ **ABOVE** The giraffes are used to hotel guests and peer right into the living room to greet them. **FACING PAGE** The entrance leads to the largest room in the house, with high arches that allow the air to circulate. The ivory-coloured walls set off the yellow wood. In the background, a chair and a footstool on a floor of local boards. Above the chimneypiece, a portrait from the 1920s. ✳ **OBEN** Die Giraffen haben sich an die Hotelgäste gewöhnt und begrüßen sie durch Fenster und Türen. **RECHTE SEITE** Durch die Eingangstür betritt man direkt den größten Raum, unter dessen Bögen die Luft zirkulieren kann. Die elfenbeinfarbenen Wände bringen das helle Holz gut zur Geltung. Im Hintergrund steht ein Sessel mit Fußstütze auf dem Parkett aus hiesigem Holz. Über dem Kamin hängt ein Porträt aus den 1920er Jahren. ✳ **CI-DESSUS** Les girafes sont habituées aux clients de l'hôtel et viennent les saluer jusque dans le salon. **PAGE DE DROITE** L'entrée donne directement sur la pièce la plus vaste de la maison avec ses arches qui permettent à l'air de circuler. Les murs ivoire mettent en valeur le bois blond. Au fond, un fauteuil et son repose-pied sur un parquet en bois local. Au-dessus de la cheminée, un portrait des années 1920.

✵ **FACING PAGE** A colonial era telephone. **ABOVE** The classic mahogany library, in perfect harmony with the English sofa, where you can take your ease after a safari in the neighbouring game park. **BELOW** A complete Art Deco bathroom. ✵ **LINKE SEITE** Ein Telefon aus der Kolonialzeit. **OBEN** Das englische Sofa passt gut in die klassisch angelegte Bibliothek aus Mahagoni. Hier kann man sich nach einer Safari im benachbarten Nationalpark ausruhen. **UNTEN** In den Bädern dominiert der Art-déco-Stil. ✵ **PAGE DE GAUCHE** Un téléphone de l'époque coloniale. **CI-DESSUS** La bibliothèque de facture classique fabriquée en acajou, s'harmonise avec le canapé anglais où l'on peut s'étendre après un safari dans le parc voisin. **CI-DESSOUS** Dans les salles de bains règne le «total look» art-déco.

Sirocco House
Lake Naivasha

This Art Deco villa built on a lake shore beloved of hippos has a past
as romantic as anything in *Out of Africa*.

Think of Mozart's music played over the harsh cries of a hippo colony. That, according to its owner, is as good a definition of Sirocco House as any.

No reference to the 1930s architecture and furnishings; no, the place itself, like an auditorium, draws its majesty from a melody that is to be found nowhere else on the planet. "When she built this property, my mother was dreaming of a space entirely dedicated to music in the middle of the bush," says Oria Douglas-Hamilton, who with her husband Ian has restored the house over a period of seven years. In the beginning there was the shared passion for Africa between an artist, Giselle Bunau-Varilla, and her Italian aviator husband Mario Rocco. The year was 1930, and the villa was built according to plans by the French modernist architect Hervé Bazin. It was a simple design: big bedrooms on the first floor surrounded by a wide veranda, a roof supported by thick octagonal cedar trunks, a living room opening on another veranda, and an estate of 3,000 hectares. The couple lived in this paradise for over 50 years. After her parents died, Oria Douglas-Hamilton picked up the gauntlet and opened her "farm" to visitors. Far from the agitation of Nairobi, life at Sirocco House still has the power to evoke the Africa of Karen Blixen.

Eine Mischung aus einer Mozartpartitur und dem Grunzen der Flusspferde – diese Beschreibung würde Sirocco House am ehesten gerecht, meint die Hausherrin selbst.

Weder die Architektur aus den 1930er Jahren noch die Einrichtung aus derselben Zeit spielen ihrer Meinung nach die Hauptrolle. Nein, der Ort leite wie ein Auditorium seine Großartigkeit von einer einzigartigen Melodie her. »Beim Bau ihres Hauses schwebte meiner Mutter ein von Musik erfüllter Ort mitten in der Savanne vor«, erklärt Oria Douglas-Hamilton, die das Gebäude gemeinsam mit ihrem Mann Ian sieben Jahre lang restauriert hat. Alles begann mit einer leidenschaftlichen Begeisterung für Afrika, die die Künstlerin Giselle Bunau-Varilla und ihren Mann, den italienischen Flieger Mario Rocco, verband. Wir schreiben das Jahr 1930, die Villa wird nach Entwürfen des französischen Architekten Hervé Bazin gebaut. Die Aufteilung ist schlicht: Eine große Veranda umgibt die geräumigen Zimmer auf der ersten Etage, dicke achteckige Zedernstämme tragen das Dach, ein Salon mit eigener Veranda – das Ganze auf einem nahezu 3000 Hektar großen Anwesen. Mehr als 50 Jahre verbringen die Eheleute in ihrem Paradies. Nach dem Tod ihrer Eltern eröffnet Oria Douglas-Hamilton eine »Farm« für Reisende, die eine gemütliche Atmosphäre schätzen. In sicherer Entfernung von der Hektik Nairobis fühlt man sich im Sirocco House in die Zeit von Karen Blixen zurückversetzt.

Une fusion entre une partition de Mozart et le chant rauque des hippopotames. Voici, selon sa propriétaire, la définition la plus juste de Sirocco House.

Aucune référence à l'architecture des années 1930 ni à l'ameublement de même époque, non, l'endroit, pareil à un auditorium, tiendrait sa majesté d'une mélodie unique au monde. «En érigeant son domaine, ma mère rêvait d'un espace dédié à la musique au milieu de la savane», confie Oria Douglas-Hamilton qui, aux côtés de son époux Ian, a restauré l'endroit pendant sept années. À l'origine, il y a la passion commune pour l'Afrique d'une artiste, Giselle Bunau-Varilla, et de son mari Mario Rocco, aviateur italien. Nous sommes en 1930, la villa est édifiée d'après les plans de l'architecte moderniste français Hervé Bazin. L'ensemble est simple: de grandes chambres à l'étage entourées d'une vaste véranda, un toit soutenu par d'épais troncs de cèdres octogonaux, un salon ouvert sur sa véranda et, surtout, un domaine de près de 3000 hectares. Le couple vit dans son paradis plus de 50 ans. Après la disparition de ses parents, Oria Douglas-Hamilton reprend le flambeau et ouvre sa «ferme» aux voyageurs épris d'intimité. Loin de l'agitation de Nairobi, vivre à Sirocco House c'est se retrouver à l'époque de Karen Blixen.

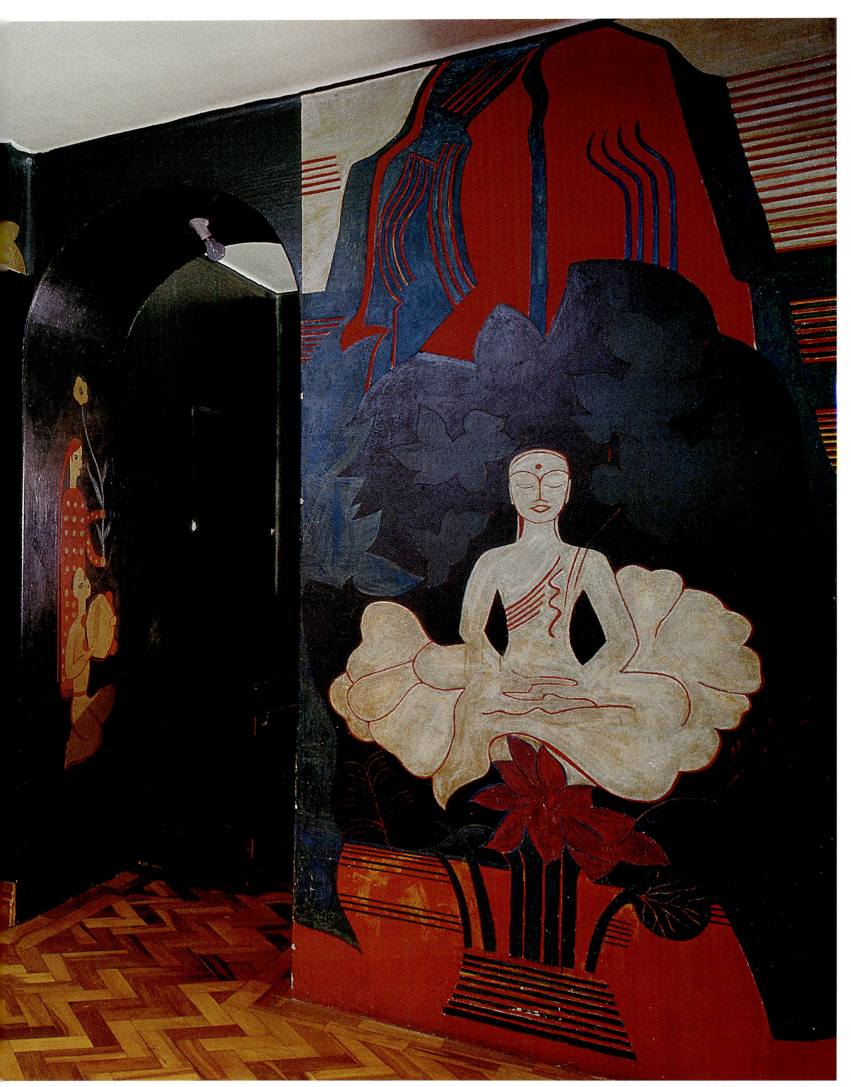

✳ **PREVIOUS PAGES** All the Art Deco furniture in the house was designed in the 1930s by Giselle Bunau-Varilla. **ABOVE** The living room still has its original Art Deco authenticity. The Afghan kilims are certified mid-19th century. ✳ **VORHERGEHENDE DOPPELSEITE** Sämtliche Art-déco-Möbel wurden in den 1930er Jahren von Giselle Bunau-Varilla entworfen. **OBEN** Der Salon im authentischen Art déco. Die afghanischen Kelims stammen verbürgtermaßen aus der Mitte des 19. Jahrhunderts. ✳ **DOUBLE PAGE PRÉCÉDENTE** Les meubles Art Déco de la maison ont tous été dessinés dans les années 1930 par Giselle Bunau-Varilla. **CI-DESSUS** Le salon garde son authenticité Art Déco. Les kilims afghans son certifiés milieu du 19ᵉ siècle.

DODO'S TOWER
LAKE NAIVASHA

An oriental pagoda in the midst of the forest.
Or rather an inhabited tree, which is how its creator sees it.

There's a strong likelihood that tourists in the centuries to come will view this brainchild of one woman, Dodo Cunningham-Reid, with the same interest that we feel nowadays for 18th century English follies.

There's something rather breathtaking about a 100-foot tower entirely furnished with European antiques in the middle of an African forest. With its cypress-wood shingles, the house is as tall as the huge acacias that surround it. And it's only a step from the vegetable to the animal world, since giraffes, gazelles, zebras and pink flamingoes, among other things, live on the 600-acre surrounding property. An architect, George Wade, working from the drawings made by Dodo Cunningham-Reid, supervised a laborious construction project that took four years to complete (the hippos that systematically laid waste the plumbing are still a burning memory). But the form of this building is more than matched by its interior. To the inherited furniture of an old English family have been added other beautiful things made in Nairobi. As a legacy to future generations, the tower is also a delight that is shared, because it is occasionally rented to amateurs of remarkable houses. In the bedroom are bunches of roses from the garden in crystal vases, the final touch of romantic luxury.

Jede Wette, dass die Touristen in den nächsten Jahrhunderten diese Ausgeburt der weiblichen Fantasie, Dodo Cunningham-Reids Meisterwerk, mit der gleichen Begeisterung betrachten werden, die wir heute der englischen Exzentrik des 18. Jahrhunderts entgegenbringen.

Schließlich ist ein 35 Meter hoher Turm mitten im afrikanischen Busch, möbliert mit europäischen Antiquitäten, durchaus etwas Besonderes. Der mit Zypressenholz verkleidete Wohnsitz versteckt sich zwischen den riesigen Akazien seiner Umgebung. Auf dem 250 Hektar großen Anwesen leben überdies Giraffen, Gazellen, Zebras und rosa Flamingos, um nur einige der Tiere zu nennen. Anhand der Zeichnungen von Dodo Cunningham-Reid wurde der Turm unter der Leitung des Architekten George Wade innerhalb von vier mühsamen Jahren gebaut. Form und Einrichtung dieser Residenz suchen ihresgleichen. Das von einer alteingesessenen englischen Familie geerbte Mobiliar wurde durch weitere in Nairobi hergestellte Möbelstücke ergänzt. Der Turm ist nicht nur ein Vermächtnis für zukünftige Generationen, bereits heute hat er Fans unter den Liebhabern außergewöhnlicher Häuser gefunden. In den Zimmern erblühen in Kristallvasen Rosen aus dem eigenen Garten – ein Detail des romantischen Luxus. Ist dies ein neuer Turm von Babel?

Il y a fort à parier que les touristes des siècles à venir visiteront ce produit de l'imagination d'une femme, Dodo Cunningham-Reid, avec le même enthousiasme que nous éprouvons aujourd'hui devant les «folies» anglaises du 18e siècle.

Il faut dire qu'une tour de 35 mètres de hauteur, en pleine forêt africaine, meublée d'antiquités européennes, a de quoi étonner. Revêtue de bois de cyprès, l'habitation joue la complémentarité avec les immenses acacias qui l'entourent. Du végétal à l'animal il n'y a qu'un pas puisque girafes, gazelles, zèbres et flamants roses, entre autres, vivent sur les 250 hectares de la propriété. C'est l'architecte George Wade qui, suivant les dessins de Dodo Cunningham-Reid, a supervisé une laborieuse construction de quatre années (on se souvient des hippopotames qui détruisaient systématiquement la plomberie!). Mais la forme de l'habitation n'a d'égale que sa décoration. Au mobilier hérité d'une vieille famille anglaise ont été ajoutées d'autres créations fabriquées à Nairobi. Legs aux générations futures, la tour est aussi un plaisir partagé, car cette «folie» est louée aux amateurs de maisons exceptionnelles. Dans les chambres, les roses du jardin, détails d'un luxe romantique, s'épanouissent dans des vases en cristal. Une nouvelle tour de Babel?

※ **PAGE 280** The great English tradition of the "folly," reinvented in an African forest. Every year the tower is re-varnished to preserve its honey colour. **ABOVE AND FACING PAGE** The staircase runs up the whole tower, which narrows towards the top and ends in the meditation room painted in *trompe l'œil* by David Merrian. ※ **SEITE 280** Im Herzen des Waldes wurde die große Tradition englischer Exzentrik wiederbelebt. Der Turm wird jedes Jahr frisch lackiert. So bewahrt er seine schöne Honigfarbe. **OBEN UND RECHTE SEITE** Die Treppe zieht sich durch den gesamten Turm, der sich nach oben hin verjüngt bis zum Meditationsraum, welcher von David Merrian im Trompe-l'œil-Stil ausgemalt wurde. ※ **PAGE 280** La grande tradition anglaise des «folies» a été réinventée au cœur de la forêt. Chaque année, la tour est revernie pour préserver sa couleur miel. **CI-DESSUS ET PAGE DE DROITE** L'escalier grimpe le long de la tour qui se rétrécit jusqu'à la salle de méditation peinte en trompe-l'œil par David Merrian.

❋ **BELOW** In this bathroom, a varnished cedar ceiling and polished mahogany panelling. On the towel rack, the linen is embroidered with the arms of the house. **FACING PAGE** A lavatory, decorated with little Chinese towers. **FOLLOWING PAGES** Breakfast, served with old crockery on a teak table. The pavilion in the trees is used as a massage room. Close to Lake Naivasha with its abundant fauna, the tower is also within reach of the Aberdare Mountains. ❋ **UNTEN** Badezimmer mit polierter Mahagonivertäfelung; die Zimmerdecke ist aus lackiertem Zedernholz. Die Bade- und Handtücher auf den Halterungen sind mit dem Wappen des Hauses bestickt. **RECHTE SEITE** Kleiner Waschraum, dekoriert mit chinesischen Türmchen. **FOLGENDE DOPPELSEITE** Großes Frühstück mit altem Geschirr auf einem Teaktisch. Der Pavillon unter den Bäumen dient als Massageraum. In der Nähe des Naivasha-Sees mit seiner großartigen Tierwelt steht der Turm in direkter Nachbarschaft zu den Bergen von Aberdare. ❋ **CI-DESSOUS** Dans cette salle de bains, cèdre verni au plafond et boiseries en acajou poli au papier de verre. Sur le porte-serviettes, le linge de maison est brodé aux armes de la maison. **PAGE DE DROITE** Cabinet de toilette décoré de petites tours chinoises. **DOUBLE PAGE SUIVANTE** Sur une table en teck, un petit-déjeuner chic dans une vaisselle ancienne. Le pavillon dans les arbres sert de salon de massage. Tout près du lac Naivasha où la faune est abondante, la tour voisine avec les montagnes de l'Aberdare.

HIPPO Point

Lake Naivasha

A cottage in Kent, vintage 1930? Not a bit of it.
Those aren't sheep, they're hippos.

Hippo Point is another vestige of the colonial era, a Tudor-style house by the architect Sir Edwin Lutyens with an English lawn in front.

The garden is geometrically perfect, the grass so impeccably cut that you'd swear it had been snipped with scissors; and the house itself, built in 1933, is now an eight bedroom hotel belonging to the owner of the magnificent Dodo's Tower (see previous pages). A few years ago, the facade was still daubed in a tar-coloured rendering. This was patiently removed by Dodo Cunningham-Reid, to reveal the kind of half-timbering that was typical of 1930s England (though in this case the wood was cedar). With her romantic pink-hued 'cottage' and its carefully decorated bedrooms, Dodo has reinvented the original style of this place, in a distinctive way that oscillates between classical and modern. The dining room furniture is teak; the china is a vestige of European aristocracy, like the linen sheets, which were made in Russia and brought to England before coming to rest in Kenya. Even the wild animals all around – antelopes, gazelles and zebras – seem to have trotted out of a romantic novel. But don't go too close – they're real enough, and sometimes they forget their manners.

Hippo Point, ein Relikt aus der Kolonialzeit mit breitem englischen Rasen, trägt den Tudor-Stil des Architekten Sir Edwin Luytens stolz zur Schau.

Der Garten ist geometrisch, der Rasen makellos wie mit der Schere geschnitten. Die 1933 erbaute Anlage beherbergt inzwischen ein Hotel mit acht Zimmern, das der Eigentümerin von Dodo's Tower gehört (siehe vorhergehende Seiten). Noch vor wenigen Jahren zierte teerfarbener Rauputz die Fassade, der von Dodo Cunningham-Reid in geduldiger Kleinarbeit entfernt wurde, bis die Balken aus Zedernholz zum Vorschein kamen, die für das edwardianische England der 1930er Jahre charakteristisch sind. Die Eigentümerin verwandelte das Gebäude in ein romantisches, rosa gestrichenes Cottage mit liebevoll eingerichteten Hotelzimmern. Heutzutage würde man es als eine gelungene Mischung aus klassischem und modernem Stil bezeichnen. Die Gäste speisen in einem Teakholz-Ambiente von altem Geschirr. Die aus Russland stammende Leinenwäsche, ein Vermächtnis der europäischen Aristokratie, wurde nach England exportiert, bevor sie schließlich nach Kenia kam. Selbst die wilden Tiere, Antilopen, Gazellen und Zebras scheinen einem romantischen Märchen entsprungen zu sein. Aber Vorsicht! Sie sind echt und haben nicht immer die besten Manieren.

Vestige de l'époque coloniale, Hippo Point arbore fièrement son habitat de tradition «Tudor» édifié devant une pelouse anglaise par l'architecte Sir Edwin Luytens.

Jardin géométrique, vert impeccable d'une herbe que l'on jurerait taillée au ciseau, ce domaine, édifié en 1933, est désormais un hôtel de huit chambres appartenant à la propriétaire de la magnifique Dodo's Tower (voir pages précédentes). Il y a quelques années, la façade était encore recouverte d'un crépi couleur goudron. Dodo Cunningham-Reid l'a patiemment ôté, faisant apparaître ces poutres en bois de cèdre typiques de l'Angleterre édouardienne des années 1930. Avec son cottage romantique aux teintes roses et ses chambres décorées avec soin, elle a même réinventé la place. Aujourd'hui, sa marque distinctive oscille entre classique et moderne. On dîne sur un mobilier en teck, dans des vaisselles anciennes, ces vestiges d'une aristocratie européenne que l'on retrouve jusqu'aux draps en lin, fabriqués en Russie, importés en Angleterre, avant d'atterrir au Kenya. Même les animaux sauvages, antilopes, gazelles, et autres zèbres semblent sortir tout droit d'un conte romantique. Mais défense de s'en approcher! Eux sont bien réels, et manquent parfois de savoir-vivre.

✳ **FACING PAGE** The Tudor style, typical of England in the 1930s, is exemplified by this hotel, built to original plans by Sir Edwin Lutyens. **ABOVE** Under the watchful eye of a French chef, the food is prepared using products from the vegetable garden, or the neighbouring farms, all of which are certified organic. ✳ **LINKE SEITE** Nach Plänen von Sir Edwin Luytens wurde dieses Hotel im Tudor-Stil errichtet, der im England der 1930er Jahre vorherrschte. **OBEN** Der französische Chefkoch sorgt dafür, dass jeder Gast nach seinen Wünschen bekocht wird. Die Lebensmittel stammen sämtlich aus biologischem Anbau, entweder aus dem eigenen Garten oder von den Bauernhöfen der Umgebung. ✳ **PAGE DE GAUCHE** Style Tudor, typique de l'Angleterre des années 1930 pour cet hôtel édifié sur les plans de Sir Edwin Luytens. **CI-DESSUS** Sous la conduite du cuisinier français, les plats sont réalisés selon les goûts de chacun à partir des produits du jardin ou dès fermes voisines, tous certifiés bio.

❋ **PREVIOUS PAGES** The best suite at Hippo Point, with its dark wood floor and dresser. **ABOVE AND FACING PAGE** All the bathroom furniture was designed by Dodo Cunningham-Reid and made by craftsmen in Nairobi. ❋ **VORHERGEHENDE DOPPELSEITE** Von der Kommode bis zum Parkett ist diese Suite in dunklem Holz ausgestattet. Sie hat die schönsten Zimmer des Hotels. **OBEN UND RECHTE SEITE** Die Einrichtung des Badezimmers wurde nach Entwürfen von Dodo Cunningham-Reid in Nairobi angefertigt. ❋ **DOUBLE PAGE PRÉCÉDENTE** Avec ses bois sombres qui courent de la commode au parquet, la suite est l'endroit privilégié de Hippo Point. **CI-DESSUS ET PAGE DE DROITE** Les meubles de la salle de bains, exécutés par des artisans de Nairobi, ont tous été dessinés par Dodo Cunningham-Reid.

Armando Tanzini
Malindi Coast

This colonnaded house open to the sea-breeze
is a delicious mix of the ethnic and the classical.

As so often happens, it was love at first sight be-tween Kenya and this particular European traveller, with art as the bridge between them.

Born in Tuscany, Armando Tanzini now pro-claims himself Italian-Kenyan because his work, which he defines as classical and primitive, straddles both continents. His house on the seashore at Malin-di, a majestic colonnaded old building with a typical East African *makuti* roof, reflects this precisely. The floors and doors were designed by Tanzini himself; the warm shades of the wooden floorboards and ceilings blend with those of the panelling and the old Chinese, Indian and Lamu furniture. The care taken with every detail here is pure delight. Like his masters Henri Ma-tisse, Pablo Picasso, Constantin Brancusi and Alberto Giacometti, Tanzini acknowledges the primacy of African sculpture, which he mixes with his own Flor-entine inheritance. Armando carries Africa in him (even his name sounds a little like Kenya's southern neigh-bour Tanzania) and he looks for an artistic rebirth in the original birthplace of mankind. It is no surprise that he defines his house as a temple of inspiration, and has started a foundation called "Do not forget Africa".

Im Leben passieren die erstaunlichsten Dinge, zum Beispiel dass sich ein europäischer Tourist für ein Land wie Kenia begeistert und eine künstlerische Verbindung herstellt.

Der gebürtige Toskaner Armando Tanzini weist sich selbst als Italo-Kenianer aus, weil sein Werk, das er als klassisch und zugleich primitiv bezeichnet, einen Spagat zwischen den Kontinenten darstellt. Sein Refugium an der Küste in Malindi beförderte diese Entwicklung. Das alte Gebäude mit dem *makuti* gedeckten, für Ostafrika charakteristischen Dach ent-faltet mit seinen vielen Säulen eine eigenartig majes-tätische Wirkung. Der Hausherr selbst gestaltete die Böden und Türen. Die warmen Farben der Bodendie-len und der Holzdecken passen gut zur Holzver-täfelung und den antiken Möbeln aus China, Indien und Lamu. Die Aufmerksamkeit für jedes Detail wird auch den Gästen zuteil. Wie seine Vorbilder Henri Matisse, Pablo Picasso, Constantin Brancusi und Alberto Giacometti pflegt der Künstler eine Vorliebe für afrikanische Skulpturen, die er mit seinem floren-tinischen Erbe kombiniert. Afrika klingt sogar in Armandos Nachnamen an (Tanzini klingt ein wenig wie Tansania, der Nachbarstaat). Er plädiert für eine Wiedergeburt der Künste, mit der die Odyssee des Homo sapiens begann. Kein Wunder, dass er diesen Ort als einen Tempel der Inspiration bezeichnet und die Stiftung »Do not forget Africa« gründete.

Comme il en existe entre les êtres, ce fut un coup de foudre entre le Kenya et un voyageur européen, avec l'art pour les réunir.

Né en Toscane, Armando Tanzini s'affiche désor-mais italo-kenyan puisque son œuvre, qu'il définit comme classique et primitive, fait le grand écart entre les continents. Pratiquement en bord de mer, son refuge de Malindi développe encore cette influence. La bâtisse ancienne au toit en *makuti*, typique des ha-bitations de l'Est africain, déploie une majesté tout en colonnes. Les sols et les portes ont été dessinés par le propriétaire. Les teintes chaudes des planchers et pla-fonds en bois se mêlent à celles des boiseries et des meubles anciens de Chine, d'Inde ou de Lamu. Le souci apporté au moindre détail transfigure le séjour des hôtes. À l'image de ses maîtres Henri Matisse, Pablo Picasso, Constantin Brancusi ou Alberto Gia-cometti, l'artiste plébiscite les sculptures africaines qu'il mêle à un patrimoine florentin. Armando porte l'Afrique jusque dans son nom (Tanzini sonne un peu comme Tanzanie, le pays voisin), pour une renais-sance des arts, là même où s'amorça l'odyssée des homos sapiens. Pas étonnant que l'endroit se définisse comme un temple de l'inspiration sous la forme d'une fondation baptisée «Do not forget Africa».

❋ **ABOVE AND FACING PAGE** A four-poster bed found in Kenya and veiled in immaculate silk. The armchair was bought in Lamu; the painting is by Armando Tanzini, in whose work the female form is a central element. ❋ **OBEN UND RECHTE SEITE** Tanzini entdeckte dieses mit strahlend weißer Seide verschleierte Himmelbett in Kenia, den Sessel fand er in Lamu. Frauenbildnisse sind ein zentrales Thema im Werk des Künstlers. ❋ **CI-DESSUS ET PAGE DE DROITE** Lit à baldaquin découvert au Kenya et voilé de soie immaculée. Fauteuil chiné à Lamu et représentation féminine, élément central du travail de l'artiste.

Katharina Schmezer & Hermann Stucki

Lamu

A riot of colours offsets the blinding white geometry of this 18th century house in the purest Swahili style.

More often than not, the purchase of a house is the result of a stroke of luck that occurs quite by chance. Towards the end of the 1970s the painter Hermann Stucki had just sold a series of drawings and collages in Nairobi.

His pockets were full of Kenyan shillings, a currency which cannot be taken out of the country. As luck would have it, he found himself in Lamu Town, a tumbledown port near the Somali border, built centuries ago in the mangrove swamp by Moorish slave traders. In the maze of streets lived a tiny cosmopolitan crowd originating from Persia, Yemen, Oman, Malaysia, India, Portugal, and the African mainland. In a quiet corner Stucki and his companion Katharina Schmezer found a house in the Arab colonial style, empty and for sale. The couple plunged into a renovation adventure that was to last for the next 15 years. In Europe, they both work, among others, for Fabric Frontline, a company specializing in finest silks, which collaborates with the most famous fashion and interior designers. Hermann designs fabric prints and Katharina represents the company in Paris. Naturally enough, the walls of their "White House" are set off by vibrant coloured fabrics, which billow in the ocean breeze. Now that their house is finished, the couple have launched themselves into the renovation of other ruins. With their excellent knowledge of the local language, they are a veritable mine of information for any newcomer who succumbs to the island's charm.

Der Kauf eines Hauses hängt oftmals mit einem unerwarteten Glückstreffer zusammen. Der Maler Hermann Stucki konnte Ende der 1970er Jahre in Nairobi unverhofft eine Reihe von Zeichnungen und Collagen verkaufen.

Als er also gerade im Besitz dieses kleinen Vermögens in kenianischen Schilling war, das er nicht ausführen durfte, entdeckte er Lamu, eine heruntergekommene Hafenstadt, die unweit der somalischen Grenze vor Jahrhunderten von Sklavenhändlern in die Mangrovensümpfe gebaut worden war. Im Labyrinth der Gassen lebte eine kleine Gemeinschaft von Kosmopoliten, die aus Persien, dem Jemen, Oman, Malaysia, Indien, Portugal und vom afrikanischen Festland stammten. An einer idyllischen Straßenecke erwartete ein Haus im arabischen Kolonialstil seine neuen Besitzer. Voller Energie stürzten sich Hermann Stucki und Katharina Schmezer in die Renovierung, ein Abenteuer, das 15 Jahre in Anspruch nehmen sollte. Das Ehepaar arbeitet unter anderem für Fabric Frontline, eine Schweizer Firma, die luxuriöse Seidenstoffe herstellt und die berühmten Modehäuser beliefert. Hermann Stucki entwirft für sie Stoffdessins, während Katharina Schmezer die Firma bei den großen Couturiers in Paris vertritt. So ist es nicht verwunderlich, dass leuchtend bunte Seidenstoffe die Wände ihres „weißen Hauses" hervorheben. Seitdem sie ihr Haus fertig gestellt haben, kümmert sich das Ehepaar um die Renovierung weiterer verfallener Häuser. Sie sprechen die Landessprache Kisuaheli und öffnen somit jedem Liebhaber der Insel Tür und Tor bei den Einheimischen.

Souvent, l'achat d'une maison procède d'un hasard heureux. Peintre, Hermann Stucki rencontre un joli succès avec une série de collages et dessins vendus à Nairobi.

À la tête d'une petite fortune en shillings kenyans, monnaie qu'il ne peut sortir du pays, il découvre, vers la fin des années 1970, Lamu Town, un port déglingué érigé il y a des siècles dans la mangrove par des négriers maures. Dans l'entrelacs de ruelles vit une petite communauté cosmopolite originaire de la Perse, du Yémen, d'Oman, de Malaisie, d'Inde, du Portugal et du continent africain. Dans un coin pittoresque, une maison de style colonial arabe attend ses nouveaux propriétaires. Hermann Stucki et Katharina Schmezer se lancent pleins d'enthousiasme dans l'aventure d'une rénovation. Une aventure qui durera 15 ans! En Europe, le couple travaille entre autres pour la maison Fabric Frontline, fabricant suisse de tissus de soie luxueux, qui collabore avec les grands couturiers et décorateurs d'intérieur. Katharina la représente sur Paris, et Hermann dessine pour ses tissus imprimés. Tout naturellement, les murs de la «maison blanche» sont relevés par les vibrantes couleurs d'étoffes gonflées par les vents marins. Leur maison achevée, le couple se lance dans l'aménagement d'autres ruines. Familiers de la langue du pays, le swahili, ils sont un sésame pour quiconque succombe aux charmes de l'île.

※ **ABOVE** The inner courtyard gives access to the main building with its three rooms in a row. The battle against humidity never ceases in Lamu; even the wall renderings have to be protected by a layer of wax. **FOLLOWING PAGES** Beside the deep well, the traditional pool, stocking water for the plants, brings a touch of modernity to the tropical garden. **PAGES 816–817** A loggia covered with plaited palm leaves filters Lamu's relentless sunshine. ※ **OBEN** Der Innenhof führt ins Hauptgebäude mit den drei hintereinander liegenden Zimmern. Der Kampf gegen die Feuchtigkeit gehört in Lamu zum Alltag, deshalb schützt eine Wachsschicht den Mauerbewurf. **FOLGENDE DOPPELSEITE** Das traditionelle Wasserbecken neben dem tiefen Ziehbrunnen dient als Reservoir zur Bewässerung und verleiht dem tropischen Garten einen modernen Akzent. **SEITEN 816–817** Eine mit Kokospalmblättern gedeckte Laube hält das mörderische Sonnenlicht ab. ※ **CI-DESSUS** Depuis la cour intérieure on accède au bâtiment principal avec ses trois pièces en alignement. Se battre contre l'humidité est une bataille sans fin à Lamu: l'enduit des murs est protégé par une couche de cire. **DOUBLE PAGE SUIVANTE** À côté du puits profond, le bassin traditionnel, qui sert de réservoir d'eau d'arrosage donne au jardin tropical une touche de modernité. **PAGES 816–817** Une tonnelle couverte de feuilles de palmes tressées filtre le soleil assassin de Lamu.

❊ **FACING PAGE AND BELOW** Hermann Stucki designed the living room furniture himself and had it made by Husseini, today the most talented carpenter in Lamu, a neighbour whom he and Katharina have known since he was a child. The beams are painted black and vermilion, native style, with white inlaid lines filled with plaster made from shell-lime. **RIGHT** The wall, pocked with 130 *zidaka* or stucco niches, is typical of feudal Swahili buildings; before the renovation work, it was covered by a thick layer of plaster. ❊ **LINKE SEITE UND UNTEN** Die Möbel im Salon hat Hermann Stucki entworfen und von seinem Nachbarn Husseini, heute der begabteste Schreiner in Lamu, den er und Katharina seit seiner Kindheit kennen, anfertigen lassen. Die Balken sind in der suahelischen Tradition schwarz und ochsenblutrot bemalt, versehen mit weißen vertieften Linien, die mit Muschelgips gefüllt sind. **RECHTS** Vor der Renovierung waren die *zidaka*, die für die feudalen Häuser oder kleinen Paläste der Suaheli typischen, in einer Mauer eingelassenen Stucknischen, hier 130 Stück, mit einer dicken Mörtelschicht zugekleistert. ❊ **PAGE DE GAUCHE ET CI-DESSOUS** Dans le salon, Hermann Stucki a lui-même dessiné des meubles fabriqués par Husseini, un voisin menuisier, aujourd'hui le plus doué à Lamu, que le couple connaît depuis son enfance. Les poutres sont peintes dans la tradition swahili en noir et vermeil, avec des sillons garnis d'un enduit blanc de poudre de coquillage. **A DROITE** Les *zidaka* sont des niches en stuc (ici au nombre de 130) creusées dans un mur des maisons féodales swahili; avant la rénovation, elles étaient recouvertes d'une épaisse couche d'enduit.

❋ **PREVIOUS PAGES** A bed of woven palm fronds. The bedcovers in the house are made of precious silks in an ethnic style, as are the curtains, hanging on 18th century wooden curtain-rails and dividing up the rooms. The floors are covered with traditional mosque-mats. **ABOVE** Shisham dresser, mirror and lamp. **FACING PAGE** This 19th century four-poster bed, found on the island, is upholstered in duchess silk, the bedcover is made from a sari. Lying by the bed is a gorgeous *mkeka*, a rare handmade Tanzanian rug made of palm fronds. ❋ **VORHER-GEHENDE DOPPELSEITE** Eine Liegestatt aus geflochtenen Palmwedeln. In diesem Haus sind die Tagesdecken und raumunterteilenden Vorhänge, die an massiven Holzstangen aus dem 18. Jahrhundert hängen, aus Seidenstoffen im Ethno-Stil gefertigt. Herkömmliche Moschee-Matten schmücken die Böden. **OBEN** Kommode, Spiegel und Lampe aus ostindischem Palisander. **RECHTE SEITE** Das Himmelbett aus dem 19. Jahrhundert stammt von der Insel selbst. Die Decke ist aus Saristoff, der Betthimmel in Duchesseseide gepatched. Unter dem Bett liegt ein wunderschöner *mkeka*, ein aus Palmwedeln handgefertigter, seltener Teppich aus Tansania. ❋ **DOUBLE PAGE PRÉCÉDENTE** Couchette en tressage de palmes séchées. Les dessus-de-lit de la maison sont réalisés dans des soieries type ethno ainsi que les rideaux, pendus sur des tringles 18e en bois massif, qui divisent les grandes pièces. Sols habillés d'une natte traditionnelle de mosquée. **CI-DESSUS** Commode, miroir et lampe en palissandre indien. **PAGE DE DROITE** Le baldaquin du lit, certifié 19e, découvert sur l'île, est habillé de soie duchesse, le couvre-lit est réalisé avec un sari. Sous le lit, un magnifique *mkeka*, tapis rare de Tanzanie tissé main à partir de feuilles de palmier.

※ **PREVIOUS PAGES, ABOVE AND RIGHT** In the kitchen, a successful marriage between the romance of a traditional house and the contemporary character of this interior, with its cement floor. The roof is surfaced with plaited coconut palmleaves. Traditional local crockery. ※ **VORHERGEHENDE DOPPELSEITE, OBEN UND RECHTS** Die Küche kombiniert die Romantik des alten Hauses mit hochmodernen Elementen, zum Beispiel dem Zementboden. Dach aus Kokospalmwedeln. Traditionelles Geschirr. ※ **DOUBLE PAGE PRÉCÉDENTE, CI-DESSUS ET À DROITE** Dans la cuisine, mariage réussi entre le romantisme d'une maison traditionnelle et la puissante touche contemporaine de son espace intérieur avec son sol en ciment. Toit en feuille de cocotier tressée. Vaisselle traditionnelle.

❋ **ABOVE** There is very little water in Lamu, therefore the bathrooms, for instance, have pools, called *birika*, to store the water. To take a shower, one draws directly from the pool by using a coconut shell ladle. ❋ **OBEN** In Lamu gibt es nicht überall fließendes Wasser. Deshalb wird es, zum Beispiel für das Badezimmer, in gemauerten Becken, den *birika* gespeichert. Daraus schöpft man direkt das Duschwasser mittels einer aus Kokosschale hergestellten Kelle. ❋ **CI-DESSUS** L'eau courante n'est pas évidente à Lamu. Dans les maisons typiques elle est stockée, par exemple à la salle de bains, dans des bassins, les *birika*. Une louche fabriquée avec une noix de coco sert à se doucher, en puisant l'eau directement du bassin.

✽ **ABOVE** Small fishes are swimming in the *birika* to keep the water clean and to eliminate the mosquito-larvae. ✽ **OBEN** In der *birika* schwimmen kleine Fische, die das Wasser sauberhalten und die Mückenlarven fressen. ✽ **CI-DESSOUS** Dans les *birika* des petits poissons gardent l'eau propre et éliminent les larves de moustiques.

Yago Casado
Lamu

This house, built in 1720 in the purest local style,
has been decorated throughout by its owner, a Spanish painter based in Milan.

Originally constructed in the 18th century, when the slave trade between Yemen and Zanzibar was at its height, this building is something of a labyrinth.

The open vestibule is a place of welcome, but also of defence. Its L-shape creates a dead end designed to resist an attack, or at least to allow a retreat back into the house. Dominated by a 100-foot tall palm tree, the latter has an interior garden, a fountain and a well of its own. This area lies to one side of a two-storey building; the ground floor area, which is characteristic of the Swahili style with its 18-foot ceiling, has beautiful columns decorated with flower motifs. There are no doors or windows; everything is wide open to the sea breeze. An outside staircase leads to the first floor; higher up, there is another large bedroom giving onto a terrace. Yago Casado says that the view across Lamu combined with the austere lines of his house have had a revelatory effect on him. "One is different in Africa. Here your identity gradually melts away and you approach a kind of spirituality. In the end, our search is not for a place to live, but a place to die."

Das Haus wurde von einem reichen Sklaven-händler erbaut – vom Jemen bis Sansibar erreichte der Sklavenhandel seinen Höhepunkt im 18. Jahrhundert.

Das Gebäude ist außergewöhnlich verschlungen und verwinkelt. In dem offenen Vorhof fühlt sich der Besucher willkommen, gleichzeitig jedoch herausgefordert. Die L-Form führt in eine Sackgasse, die im Falle eines Angriffs die Feinde aufhalten und den Bewohnern erlauben sollte, ins Haus zu flüchten. Vor dem Gebäude steht eine 35 Meter hohe Palme und im Innenhof erblüht ein Garten mit Fontäne und eigenem Brunnen. Darüber liegt das zweistöckige Wohnhaus. Im Erdgeschoss mit seinen für den Suaheli-Stil charakteristischen, sechs Meter hohen Decken ragen stolze, mit Blumenmustern verzierte Säulen in die Höhe. Türen und Fenster gibt es nicht – der Seewind weht ungehindert durchs Haus. Eine Außentreppe führt in die erste Etage. Ein Stockwerk höher befinden sich die Terrasse und ein weiterer großer Raum. Mit Blick auf Lamu gesteht Yago Casado freimütig, dass ihm die Strenge seiner Behausung neue Sehweisen erschließt. »In Afrika wird man ein Anderer«, sagt er. »Hier löst sich die Identität langsam aber sicher auf, man nähert sich einer gewissen Spiritualität. Genau genommen sucht man nicht etwa einen Platz zum Leben, sondern einen Ort zum Sterben.« Liebe auf den ersten Blick? Das kann man wohl sagen!

Construit par un riche négrier (la traite des Noirs connut au 18e siècle son apogée entre le Yémen et Zanzibar), l'édifice impose d'emblée ses méandres.

Le vestibule ouvert accueille le visiteur, mais le défie aussi. Sa forme en L forme un cul-de-sac destiné à résister en cas d'attaque, ou tout au moins à se réfugier dans l'habitation. Dominée par un palmier de 35 mètres, celle-ci est agrémentée d'un jardin intérieur, d'une fontaine et d'un puits. Ce passage est situé à l'orée du bâtiment de deux étages. L'espace du rez-de-chaussée, caractéristique du style swahili avec ses 6 mètres sous plafond, arbore des colonnes décorées de motifs floraux. Ni portes ni fenêtres – l'ensemble est ouvert au vent marin. Un escalier extérieur grimpe au premier étage. Plus haut, la terrasse abrite encore une grande chambre. D'ici, avec vue sur Lamu, Yago Casado confie volontiers que les lignes austères de sa demeure agissent sur lui comme un révélateur. «On est différent en Afrique», dit-il. «Ici, l'identité se dissout progressivement, on se rapproche d'une certaine spiritualité. En fin de compte, on ne cherche pas un endroit pour vivre, mais un endroit pour mourir.» Un coup de foudre? C'est peut dire!

❋ **ABOVE AND FACING PAGE** As soon as you enter, there is a striking contrast between the silence of the palace and the chaos outside. The first floor and terrace are at the top of an outside staircase. **FOLLOWING PAGES** From the *sundani*, or inner courtyard, you enter the main salon with its ebony furniture made in Lamu. ❋ **OBEN UND RECHTS** Kaum ist man eingetreten, umgibt einen die Stille des Hofes – ein harter Kontrast zum Lärm der Gassen rundum. **FOLGENDE DOPPELSEITE** Aus dem *sundani*, dem Innenhof, tritt man in den großen Salon, der mit kargen Ebenholzmöbeln aus Lamu eingerichtet ist. ❋ **CI-DESSOUS ET PAGE DE DROITE** Dès l'entrée, la cour impose un contraste entre le silence du palais et le chaos des ruelles. On grimpe à l'étage et à la terrasse par un escalier extérieur. **DOUBLE PAGE SUIVANTE** Depuis le *sundani*, la cour intérieure, on pénètre dans le grand salon au sobre mobilier en bois d'ébène fabriqué à Lamu.

※ **ABOVE** On the walls are paintings of Arab traders by Yago Casado. **FACING PAGE** The artist's studio. **FOLLOWING PAGES** In the chambers formerly reserved for the father and eldest son of the family, note the lovely Swahili baby cradle and the *zidaka* alcoves above the beds. On the floor, a Jambi palm mat. ※ **OBEN** Die Bilder von Yago Casado stellen arabische Händler dar. **RECHTE SEITE** Das Atelier des Malers. **FOLGENDE DOPPELSEITE** In den Zimmern, die früher Vater und Sohn vorbehalten waren, befindet sich eine schöne suahelische Wiege. Oberhalb der Betten sind die typischen Nischen – *zidaka* genannt, auf dem Boden liegt ein Teppich aus Palmenfasern. ※ **CI-DESSUS** Aux murs, les tableaux signés Yago Casado représentent des marchands arabes. **PAGE DE DROITE** L'atelier du peintre. **DOUBLE PAGE SUIVANTE** Dans les chambres autrefois réservées au père et au fils de la famille, on remarque un beau berceaux swahili.

❋ **ABOVE** One of the painter's models, carefully posed in his traditional dress. **FACING PAGE** The house has three bathrooms, all restored in the style of the island. The beams in the ceiling are painted black, white and vermilion in the Swahili tradition. ❋ **OBEN** Das Modell des Malers ist nach einheimischer Art geschmückt und gekleidet. **RECHTE SEITE** Die drei Bäder des Hauses wurden im Stil der Insel restauriert. Die Deckenbalken sind in den Farben der Suaheli Schwarz, Weiß und Karminrot gestrichen. ❋ **CI-DESSOUS** Le modèle, coiffé et paré de son habit traditionnel, pose pour le peintre. **PAGE DE DROITE** La maison abrite trois salles de bains restaurées dans l'esprit de l'île. Au plafond, les poutres sont peintes dans la tradition swahilie de noir, blanc et vermeil.

Salomé's Garden

Ngorongoro Crater Lodge

Mnemba Island Lodge

Emerson & Green

TANZANIA

Ngorongoro Crater Lodge

Ngorongoro Conservation Area

This extraordinary palace stands at the lip of one of the world's oldest volcanoes.

What on earth are they doing here, these minarets among the prowling carnivores? Where are we? There's nothing else anywhere near, and the Cessna has been in the air for 45 minutes since leaving the airport.

How can we explain such a folly, seen from an altitude of 8000 feet? In the beginning was the ambition of the Conservation Corporation Africa (ccafrica.com) to install itself in the continent's most magnificent places. Then there was a meeting between two men, the architect Silvio Rech and the decorator Chris Brown. It took them a year and a force of 450 Tanzanian workers and craftsmen to create this masterpiece, which is doubtless the most beautiful hotel in Africa. Amazingly, most of the Lodge, from its structural elements to the details of its interior, was made on the spot. There was a carpentry shop for the woodwork (*mnenga* walls, *mokoro* floors), a smithy for the metals, and so on – right down to details like the copper-coil chandeliers plaited by an assembly of Masai. In the evenings, the sense of mirage returns when a troop of Masai spearmen appear in their traditional dress. And in the morning thousands of flamingos take wing against the sunrise.

Ist das eine Erscheinung? Wozu dienen mitten im Busch diese seltsamen Minarette? Wo sind wir gelandet? Rundherum nichts – nach einem 45-minütigen Flug mit der Cessna von einem kleinen Flughafen aus.

Begonnen hat alles mit dem Ehrgeiz der Conservation Corporation Africa (ccafrica.com), sich an einem der schönsten Orte Afrikas niederzulassen. Dann begegneten sich zwei Männer: der Architekt Silvio Rech und der Dekorateur Chris Brown. Sie brauchten ein Jahr und 450 tansanische Arbeiter und Handwerker für die Verwirklichung dieses Meisterwerks, des wahrscheinlich schönsten Hotels in Afrika. Dabei ist die gesamte Lodge vom Aufbau bis zur kleinsten Dekoration direkt auf der Baustelle entstanden. Die Schreinerei war für die Holzvertäfelung zuständig (Wände in *mnenga*, Parkett in *mokoro*), die Kunstschmiede bis ins Detail für die Metallarbeiten, beispielsweise für die Kronleuchter aus Kupferdraht, die von einer Gruppe Massai hergestellt wurden. In der Abenddämmerung glaubt man weiter an Wunder, wenn aus dem Busch diese Krieger auftauchen – eine Lanze in der Hand, in voller Tracht – und morgens Tausende von rosa Flamingos aus dem Krater in die aufgehende Sonne fliegen.

On dirait une apparition. Mais que viennent faire ici, au voisinage des grands fauves, ces étranges minarets? Où sommes-nous? Rien alentour, le Cesna a volé 45 minutes depuis le petit aéroport.

Comment expliquer une telle folie à 2400 mètres d'altitude? À l'origine, il y a l'ambition de la Conservation Corporation Africa (ccafrica.com), décidée à s'implanter dans les plus beaux espaces d'Afrique. Et puis cette rencontre entre deux hommes, Silvio Rech, architecte, et Chris Brown, décorateur. Il leur a fallu une année et la force de travail de 450 ouvriers et artisans tanzaniens pour réaliser ce chef-d'œuvre, peut-être le plus bel hôtel d'Afrique. Étonnamment, l'ensemble du Lodge, de sa structure à la décoration intérieure, a été fabriqué sur les pentes même du chantier. L'atelier menuiserie s'est occupé des boiseries (murs en *mnenga*, parquet en *mokoro*), l'atelier ferronnerie des métaux, et ainsi de suite jusqu'aux plus infimes détails comme ces lustres en fil de cuivre tressés par une assemblée de Massaï. À la nuit tombée, la sensation de mirage se poursuit lorsque apparaissent ces guerriers de la brousse, lance à la main, en grande tenue traditionnelle. Au matin, dans le cratère, des milliers de flamants roses s'envolent dans le soleil naissant.

✳ **PAGE 344** Comfortable English sofas, a Venetian chandelier and *mnenga* panels. **FACING PAGE** The banana leaf ceilings lend a note of exoticism to this baroque ethnic décor. ✳ **SEITE 344** Bequeme englische Sofas, ein Kronleuchter im venezianischen Stil und *mnenga*-Holzvertäfelungen. **RECHTE SEITE** Die mit Blättern der Bananenstaude verkleideten Decken verleihen der barocken Einrichtung einen Hauch von Exotik. ✳ **PAGE 344** Confort à l'anglaise: des canapés, un lustre de style vénitien et des boiseries en *mnenga*. **PAGE DE DROITE** Les plafonds en feuille de bananier donnent une touche exotique à ce décor baroque ethnique.

※ **PREVIOUS PAGES** In the dining room, the ceilings decorated with mirrors and gilded metal sunbursts were designed by the architect Silvio Rech. Under the great glass-bead chandeliers, the chairs are all upholstered with cotton damask. **ABOVE** The zinc basins have mirrors edged with gold leaf. ※ **VORHERGEHENDE DOPPELSEITE** Die Decken des Esszimmers sind mit Spiegeln und vergoldeten Metallsonnen verkleidet – eine Idee von Silvio Rech. Die Stühle unter den gläsernen Kronleuchtern wurden mit Baumwolldamast bezogen. **OBEN** Die Spiegel über den Waschbecken aus Zink sind mit Blattgold verziert. ※ **DOUBLE PAGE PRÉCÉDENTE** Dans la salle à manger, les plafonds ornés de miroirs et de soleils en métal doré ont été dessinés par l'architecte Silvio Rech. Sous les grands lustres à pampilles de verre, les chaises sont habillées de damassé de coton. **CI-DESSUS** Les lavabos en zinc sont ornés de miroirs dorés à la feuille.

※ **ABOVE** A mirror found in a London flea market. **FACING PAGE** The bathtubs, each embellished with a piece of carved wood, are set in concrete. On the walls are wooden panels attached with big nails hammered out in the Lodge's workshop. ※ **OBEN** Ein Spiegel vom Londoner Flohmarkt. **RECHTE SEITE** Die in einen Betonblock eingelassenen Badewannen sind mit Holz-schnitzerei verziert. Die Holzpaneele sind mit starken Nägeln (aus den Werkstätten der Lodge) an den Wänden befestigt. ※ **CI-DESSUS** Miroir chiné aux Puces de Londres. **PAGE DE DROITE** Les baignoires ornées d'une pièce de bois ciselé sont intégrées dans un bloc de béton. Au mur, des panneaux de bois césuré sont fixés par de gros clous, martelés dans les ateliers du Lodge.

❊ **ABOVE** A bedroom with its banana leaf ceiling. The bed is very broad, inspired by the Indian and Arabian art of neighbouring Zanzibar. ❊ **OBEN** Ein Schlafzimmer unter einem Dach aus Blättern der Bananenstaude. Das große Bett kombiniert Stilelemente der indischen und arabischen Kultur der nah gelegenen Insel Sansibar. ❊ **CI-DESSOUS** Une chambre blottie sous les feuilles de bananier. Un large lit inspiré des arts indien et arabe de l'île voisine de Zanzibar.

※ **FOLLOWING PAGES** A breakfast table, with chairs of brightly-coloured cotton velours. The view takes in the crater, with bush country in the foreground. ※ **FOLGENDE DOPPELSEITE** Man frühstückt mit Blick auf den Krater und den Busch. Die Stühle sind mit Baumwollsamt in leuchtenden Farben bezogen. ※ **DOUBLE PAGE SUIVANTE** Le petit-déjeuner sur des chaises habillées de velours de coton aux teintes vives est servi avec vue sur le cratère et la brousse.

SALOME'S GARDEN

ZANZIBAR

This *bububu* beside the sea owes its romantic touch to a princess
whose memory is still very much alive here.

The property consists of 20 acres of gardens and plantations that slope to the sea, all of which is encircled by a wall of coral. Beyond the massive wooden door is the former residence of Princess Salomé, the daughter of Sultan Busaid, who was the "king of cloves" in the mid-19th century.

Salomé, who became a bourgeois lady after she fell in love with a German businessman, was the first Muslim woman to write an autobiography. Everyone here has read her *Memoirs of an Arab Princess from Zanzibar*, a nostalgic work that describes this splendid abode with its old furniture and carpets and its broad verandas opening onto a pure white beach. The palace still stands with its arches, 10 kilometres north of Stone Town, a reminder of the island's past when the court of the Sultan of Oman made Zanzibar the capital of his empire. Faded images, which evoke a time when this offshoot of the African continent was called the Venice of the Indian Ocean, when Portuguese, Arabs, British, Indians – and even David Livingstone himself – passed through here, on their way east or west. Today Zanzibar is an island of all races and religions. A final detail: the villa can be rented by visitors.

Die Besitzung ist von acht Hektar zum Meer hin abfallenden Gärten und Plantagen umgeben und mit Korallenmauern geschützt. Hinter dem Portal liegt die frühere Residenz von Prinzessin Salme, der Tochter des Sultans Said Busaid, der Mitte des 19. Jahrhunderts als unangefochtener König der Gewürznelken galt.

Salme, die zu einer Bürgerlichen degradiert wurde, nachdem sie sich in einen deutschen Geschäftsmann verliebt hatte, erzählte als erste Muslimin ihre Lebensgeschichte. Hier gehört ihr Buch *Leben im Sultanspalast. Memoiren aus dem 19. Jahrhundert* zur Standardlektüre. Darin wird ihr zehn Kilometer von Stone Town gelegener Wohnsitz beschrieben, die Einrichtung mit antiken Möbeln und Teppichen, die großen Veranden, die auf den Strand hinausgehen. Die gotischen Gewölbe beschwören die Geschichte der Insel in jener Epoche, als der Hof des Sultans von Oman Sansibar zur Hauptstadt des Reiches erklärte. Verblichene Bilder aus jener Zeit, als dieser Zipfel des afrikanischen Kontinents zum »Venedig am Indischen Ozean« erklärt wurde und Portugiesen, Araber, Engländer, Inder und nicht zuletzt David Livingstone Sansibar besuchten. Inzwischen lebt die Insel im toleranten Einklang verschiedenster Rassen und Religionen. Ein letztes Detail: Die Villa wird an Touristen vermietet, die sich wie ein Prinz und Robinson gleichzeitig fühlen wollen.

Entourée de huit hectares de jardin et de plantations qui descendent vers la mer, la propriété est ceinte d'une muraille en pierre de corail. Passé le portail de bois massif, voici l'ancienne résidence de la princesse Salomé, la fille du sultan Saïd Busaid qui fut le roi du clou de girofle au milieu du 19e siècle.

Salomé, devenue bourgeoise après être tombée amoureuse d'un homme d'affaires allemand, fut la première femme musulmane à raconter sa vie. Tout le monde ici connaît son livre, *Mémoires d'une princesse arabe*, œuvre nostalgique qui magnifie cette demeure splendide, décorée de meubles anciens et de tapis, aux grandes vérandas qui s'ouvrent sur une plage de sable blanc. À une dizaine de kilomètres au nord de Stone Town, ces arcs en ogive rappellent l'histoire de l'île, l'époque où la cour du sultan d'Oman avait établi Zanzibar comme capitale de son empire. Des images fanées qui évoquent le temps où ce versant du continent africain était appelé «la Venise de l'océan Indien» et où les Portugais, les Arabes, les Anglais, les Indiens et David Livingstone passaient par Zanzibar. Aujourd'hui, l'île vit au rythme de tous les métissages, de toutes les religions. Dernier détail: la villa est louée à quelques touristes qui veulent jouer à la fois les princes et les Robinson.

Emerson & Green
Zanzibar

The Sultan of Oman's palace, restored with deep respect for the blend of cultures and religions which epitomizes Zanzibar.

The past of this building is closely associated with an extravagant period of the 19th century when Zanzibar reached the height of its prosperity under the sultans.

Built around the traditional enclosed garden of a Moorish palace, it is a marriage of different styles, with lacy balconies, galleries of fretted wood, and round-topped window embrasures encrusted with coloured glass. Arthur Rimbaud, among others, was fascinated by Zanzibar, though he never came here; and the Emerson & Green house has retained much of what the great French poet dreamed of. The new owners have imported some novelties. In the bedrooms, coloured cement floors contrast with dark wooden furniture, and in the mazy passageways the walls change colour half way up, while the rounded vaulting is painted in pastel shades. The island breeze has carried the heavy scent of spices for centuries past, and it still invades the tall, square building. All around, the ruins of Stone Town are gradually coming to life and every year new arrivals come to decorate them.

Die Geschichte des Hauses ist mit der des 19. Jahrhunderts eng verknüpft, als Sansibar unter der Herrschaft des Sultans von Oman eine Epoche großen Wohlstands erlebte.

Wie bei maurischen Palästen üblich, wurde das Gebäude um den traditionellen Garten im Innenhof erbaut und verbindet die unterschiedlichsten Stilrichtungen miteinander, wie Balkone mit Holzspitzenbrüstung, Gänge mit festonierter Holzspitze und oben abgerundete, grün bemalte Fenster bezeugen. Der Zauber dieser glorreichen Vergangenheit – gern besungen von romantischen Dichtern wie Arthur Rimbaud, der, obwohl er nie in Sansibar war, dennoch ständig den Namen der Insel im Munde führte – wurde für die Gegenwart bewahrt und um moderne Impulse ergänzt. In den Zimmern kontrastieren farbige Zementböden mit dunklen Holzmöbeln. Im Labyrinth der Winkel und Ecken wechseln die Wände auf halber Höhe die Farbe, während die Rundung der Rippengewölbe in Pastellfarbe erscheint. Schwere Düfte und würzige Aromen, die seit Jahrhunderten vom Inselwind hergetragen werden, strömen in das hohe viereckige Haus. Inzwischen werden nach diesem Vorbild weitere Häuser in Stone Town wieder hergerichtet. Jährlich kommen neue Antiquitätenhändler, um sie neu zu dekorieren.

La mémoire de la maison est chevillée aux fastes du 19e siècle, époque de grande prospérité pour Zanzibar, celle du règne des sultans d'Oman.

Édifiée autour du traditionnel jardin intérieur des palais maures, elle marie de nombreux styles avec ses balcons de bois dentelés, ses galeries festonnées de dentelles de bois, et ses ouvertures arrondies incrustées de verre coloré. De ce temps révolu, chanté par les écrivains romantiques, notamment par Arthur Rimbaud, qui n'y vint jamais mais qui ne cessait de répéter le nom de Zanzibar, l'Emerson & Green a conservé les attraits. Pourtant, et c'est encore là une affaire de charme, les nouveaux propriétaires ont apporté ici et là quelques traces des temps nouveaux. Dans les chambres, les sols de ciment coloré contrastent avec les meubles en bois foncé. Dans les dédales des couloirs, les murs changent de couleur à mi-hauteur et l'arrondi des ogives est peint dans des couleurs pastel. Et puis les parfums lourds et les saveurs épicées, portés depuis des siècles par le vent de l'île, envahissent la haute maison carrée. Autour d'elle, à son image, les ruines de Stone Town se redressent. Et, chaque année, de nouveaux antiquaires viennent les décorer.

※ **PREVIOUS PAGES** In the bedroom suite, the carved wooden furniture typical of Zanzibar, along with touches of colour from the rounded windows and stained glass. Traditional Zanzibar wooden bed, with its mattress nearly three feet from the floor. **ABOVE** The bathtub is made of coloured and polished cement. ※ **VORHERGEHENDE DOPPELSEITE** Die Holzschnitzerei in der Suite ist charakteristisch für Sansibar. Farbkontraste mit den abgerundeten Fenstern. Zirka ein Meter hohes traditionelles Holzbett aus Sansibar. **OBEN** Die Badewanne ist aus gefärbtem und poliertem Beton. ※ **DOUBLE PAGE PRÉCÉDENTE** Dans la suite, des meubles en bois ciselé typique de Zanzibar. Touches colorées avec des fenêtres arrondies à vitraux. Lit en bois traditionnel de Zanzibar avec son sommier perché à près d'un mètre du sol. **CI-DESSUS** La baignoire de la salle de bains est en béton teinté et poli.

MNEMBA ISLAND LODGE
near Zanzibar

On this private island, the world's most exclusive Robinson Crusoes go barefoot in the sunshine.

This is a place where you can jog along very well with just a few books, fewer clothes, and a man or woman Friday in attendance.

What you'll have as backup is the maximum luxury of this African seaside hotel. Imagine an atoll in turquoise waters protected by a barrier of coral – and ten bungalows built in the tradition of Zanzibar fishermen's huts, with decoration entirely entrusted to local artisans. The benches are made of coconut wood and hemp. The roofs and walls of the bungalows were mostly plaited on the spot. What could be more simple and luxurious? You can walk round the island in 20 minutes. There are no cars, no scorpions and no malarial mosquitoes – nothing but white sand and palm trees. Out to sea, closely ranked schools of dolphins weave their way among the multicoloured sailing dhows, playing and leaping. In the evening you lie around on white cotton poufs and talk about the exotic fishes you saw that afternoon, or – if you're lucky – the whales that throng around Mnemba in the mating season. Whales are a sign of good fortune on this African side of the Indian Ocean.

Auf Mnemba Island braucht man nur Bücher, zwei, drei Kleider und natürlich einen »Freitag« – egal welchen Geschlechts.

Das afrikanische Luxushotel liegt direkt am Strand, auf einem Atoll im türkisfarbenen Meer, geschützt von einem vorgelagerten Korallenriff. Auf der Insel stehen zehn Bungalows im Stil der Fischerhütten von Sansibar, die von den Handwerkern der Umgebung gebaut wurden. Die Liegestühle werden aus Kokosholz und Hanfseilen gefertigt. Dächer und Wände der Bungalows aus Palmenblättern werden teilweise direkt vor Ort geflochten. Kann man sich Luxus schlichter vorstellen? Die Insel ist zu Fuß in 20 Minuten umrundet, es gibt weder Autos noch Skorpione noch Malaria – nur weißen Sand und Palmen. Auf hoher See, zwischen den Daus aus Sansibar, diesen Segelbooten mit buntem Rumpf, schwimmen Delphine in dichten Schwärmen. Einer nach dem anderen springt verspielt aus dem Wasser. Abends sitzt man zusammengesunken auf einem mit weißer Baumwolle gepolsterten Hocker und erzählt von den bunten Fischen, die man am Nachmittag gesehen hat oder, wenn man richtig Glück hatte, von den Walen, die während der Paarungszeit mit Mnemba flirten. Ein gutes Omen im Indischen Ozean, der die afrikanischen Küsten umspielt.

On vit ici avec quelques livres, deux ou trois vêtements, sans oublier, à portée de main, Vendredi – homme ou femme.

Luxe maximal pour cet hôtel africain de bord de mer. Imaginez un atoll aux eaux turquoise protégées par une barrière de corail. Dix bungalows construits dans la tradition des maisons de pêcheurs de Zanzibar. Une décoration confiée aux artisans des villages voisins. Les bancs sont en bois de cocotier et en corde de chanvre. Les toits et les murs de bungalows en feuille de palme sont en partie tressés sur place. Peut-on rêver plus luxueuse simplicité? On fait le tour de l'île en 20 minutes à pied. Il n'y a ni voitures ni scorpions ni paludisme ... rien que du sable blanc et des palmiers. Au large, entre les *dhows* (boutres) de Zanzibar, ces voiliers à coques en bois multicolores, des dauphins filent en bandes serrées et sautent à la queue leu leu. Le soir, affalé sur un pouf de coton blanc, on parle des poissons multicolores observés dans l'après-midi ou – pour les plus chanceux – des baleines qui flirtent avec Mnemba pendant la saison des amours. De bon augure dans cet océan Indien qui caresse les côtes de l'Afrique.

❊ **ABOVE** A glass bead shower curtain made at Kitengela. **BELOW** *Mkadi*, a local fruit, and Kitengela carafes. **FACING PAGE** In the bedrooms, thatched roofs and coconut-wood furniture designed by the decorator Chris Brown.   ❊ **OBEN** Duschvorhang aus Glasperlen, hergestellt in Kitengela. **UNTEN** Ein *mkadi*, eine Frucht, und Karaffen aus Kitengela. **RECHTE SEITE** Der Dekorateur Chris Brown richtete die Zimmer ein: Bananenblattdächer und Kokosholzmöbel.   ❊ **EN HAUT** Rideau de douche en perles de verre fabriqué à Kitengela. **EN BAS** Le *mkadi*, un fruit de la région, et des carafes de Kitengela. **PAGE DE DROITE** Dans les chambres, toit en feuille de bananier et mobilier en cocotier dessiné avec simplicité par le décorateur Chris Brown.

Maison de Beau Séjour

Various Houses ✳

SEYCHELLES, MAURITIUS, LA RÉUNION

Salim Currimjee

Maison Folio

various
HOUSES
SEYCHELLES

These colonial houses are beautiful in their simplicity
and their promise of good living.

The *cases* built of wood or uncut stone in the Seychelles are the heritage of French and British colonial times.

By tradition, visitors are invited onto their broad, shady verandas to sit in a planter's chair and talk. A glance at the rattan furniture and the colonnades of tropical *sapele* wood and you immediately understand the logic that has guided the island's builders for centuries past: why, for instance, there are comparatively few closed-in spaces here, and why there are so many windows. The insides of the *cases* are as bare as possible, constantly refreshed by the sea breezes, while the heat of the sun is kept out by wooden lattice blinds. There are marble floors, straw mats and in the more primitive constructions *latanier* thatched roofs overhead. The Mahé museum, open to the public, offers the best example of a colonial building as one might have imagined it in the late 18th century. The little fishermen's houses and their small plots of garden are just as traditional; but they are scattered over the wild hills, and their horizon consists of the turquoise sea and a lavender-blue sky. They are entirely at one with the vegetation, the white sand, the coconut trees and the *takamakas* by the water.

Schon von der Veranda der Häuser aus Holz oder unbehauenem Stein werden die Spuren der französischen oder englischen Kolonisation offensichtlich.

Tradition verpflichtet, deshalb werden Besucher auf der schattigen Freitreppe in einen Sessel für Plantagenbesitzer genötigt. An den traditionellen Korbmöbeln und den Säulengängen mit Pfeilern aus *sapele*, einem Tropenholz, wird ersichtlich, nach welchen Prinzipien seit Jahrhunderten auf der Insel gebaut wird. Es gibt nur wenige geschlossene Räume, dafür überall Fensteröffnungen – die karg möblierten Innenräume lassen dem frischen Seewind genügend Spielraum. Klappläden aus Holzlatten schützen die Zimmer. Hier und da trifft man auf Marmor, Stroh und auf Latanienholzdächer, die die einfachsten Behausungen decken. Das Museum von Mahé ist ein hervorragendes Beispiel für die Kolonialbauweise im 18. Jahrhundert. Der Blick von den in den beinahe unberührten Hügeln verstreuten Häuser geht auf das türkisfarbene Meer hinaus, das sich unter einem lavendelblauen Himmel bis zum Horizont erstreckt. Die Gebäude verschmelzen mit der Landschaft, dem weißen Sand, den Kokospalmenalleen und den *takamaka*-Bäumen am Strand.

Découvertes depuis leur véranda, ces «cases» en bois ou pierre brute témoignent des années de colonisation française et britannique.

Tradition oblige, c'est sur ce large perron ombragé que le visiteur est invité à s'asseoir sur un fauteuil de planteur. Un coup d'œil aux meubles traditionnels en rotin, aux colonnades de piliers en *sapele*, un bois tropical, et instantanément apparaît la logique reprise depuis des siècles par les bâtisseurs de l'île: les espaces clos sont rares, les ouvertures sont partout privilégiées, les intérieurs s'animent dans leur nudité à la brise rafraîchissante de l'air marin. Les pièces sont protégées par des persiennes en lattes de bois. On retrouve ici et là du marbre, de la paille et, au-dessus des têtes, les toits de latanier recouvrent les demeures les plus sauvages. Le musée de Mahé, ouvert au public, offre le meilleur exemple d'une demeure coloniale telle qu'on l'imaginait à la fin du 18e siècle. Les petites maisons de bois de pêcheur avec leur humble jardin sont tout aussi traditionnelles. Disséminées sur les collines sauvages, elles ont pour horizon le turquoise de la mer et un ciel bleu lavande. Ces habitations forment un tout avec la végétation, le sable blanc, les allées de cocotiers et les *takamaka* bordant les rivages.

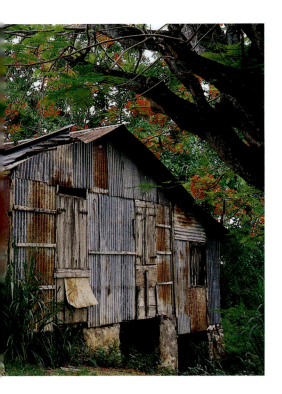

MAISON DE BEAU SÉJOUR

Mauritius

A colonial house in the north of the island has become a refined retreat that draws on several different periods.

Balanced between the ravine and the mountains, backing onto the tropical forest where ebonies and other exotic trees blend with azaleas and aromatic shrubs, Beau Séjour (as the house of the Lagesse family is called) is a testimony to the Creole life of not so long ago and the colonial epoch that reached its height in the 19th century.

Built by a Frenchman (the island had been French since the time of Louis XIV), the life of the property revolved around its immense sugar cane and banana plantations. Just as it did in Louisiana, the planter's existence so far away from the great cities of civilization led to the creation of a singular *art de vivre*. At Beau Séjour, with its traditional *varangue* (veranda) and openwork shutters to let in the cooling breezes, the façade has the look of a small palace of the kind that can still be seen from Italy to Istanbul. It is perfectly symmetrical, with carved balustrades, a comfortable *varangue* where one can sit and talk midway between house and garden, high windows, heavy shutters and light colours. The interior, recently refitted by the decorator Martine Lagesse, gives a sense of strength and finesse which is heightened by the warm, dark wood surfaces and the hunting trophies on the walls. There is a classical feel about this house which calls to mind a period engraving – or perhaps the novel *Paul et Virginie*.

Beau Séjour, so heißt das Haus der Familie Lagesse, liegt eingebettet zwischen einer kleinen Schlucht auf der einen Seite und einer Gebirgskette auf der anderen. Es schmiegt sich an einen Tropenwald, in dem zwischen Ebenholzbäumen mit Makaken darin und anderen wertvollen Hölzern Azaleensträucher und Dufthölzer stehen – ein Zeugnis der Kolonialzeit, die im 19. Jahrhundert ihren Höhepunkt erreichte.

Die von einem Franzosen gegründete Besitzung (Mauritius stand seit der Regentschaft Ludwig XIV. unter französischer Herrschaft) ist umgeben von Zuckerrohrfeldern und Bananenplantagen. Wie in Louisiana weckte die Entfernung von der modischen Welt der Städter unter den Plantagenbesitzern den Wunsch nach einem eigenen Lebensstil. Die Fassade mit der traditionell offenen Veranda und den Lamellenläden, die stets eine frische Brise durchlassen, gibt dem Haus den Anschein jener kleinen Palais, die damals von Italien bis Istanbul verbreitet waren. Eine perfekte Symmetrie der Formen, holzgeschnitzte Balustraden, eine freundliche offene Veranda, die zu Gesprächen zwischen Haus und Garten einlädt, hohe Fenster mit schweren Läden, das Ganze in hellen Farben – so vervollständigt sich das Bild. Die Dekorateurin Martine Lagesse hat die Innenräume neu gestaltet, sodass ein Eindruck von Finesse und Kraft entsteht, der die Wirkung des dunklen Holzes und der Jagdtrophäen noch hervorhebt: klassizistisch wie auf einem alten Stich. Oder aus dem Roman »Paul und Virginie«.

Entre la ravine et la chaîne de montagnes, adossée à une forêt tropicale dans laquelle les ébéniers où s'agitent des macaques et d'autres bois précieux se mêlent aux azalées et aux bois de senteur, Beau Séjour, c'est le nom de cette maison de la famille Lagesse, témoigne de la vie créole d'autrefois, cette époque coloniale qui connut son apogée au 19e siècle.

Édifié par un Français (l'île était française depuis Louis XIV), le domaine vivait tout autour de sa raison d'être: d'immenses champs de canne à sucre et plantations de bananiers. Être planteur, comme en Louisiane, éveillait chez ces sujets éloignés des modes citadines un acharnement à créer un art de vivre. Flanquée de la traditionnelle varangue et des persiennes à claire-voie qui dispensent encore une brise bienfaisante, la façade a des allures de petit palais, tels qu'on les édifiait autrefois de l'Italie à Istanbul. Symétrie parfaite des formes, balustrades ciselées, varangue confortable où l'on discute entre maison et jardin, hautes fenêtres, volets lourds, couleurs claires, voilà pour l'inspiration générale. L'intérieur, recomposé par la décoratrice Martine Lagesse, émane une impression de finesse et de force que décuplent la chaleur des bois sombres et les trophées de chasse. Un classicisme qui semble tout droit sorti d'une gravure. Ou du roman *Paul et Virginie*.

❋ **ABOVE** From the front hall, the wooden staircase and polished furniture. **FACING PAGE** Naval carpenters from France introduced the concept of the open porch to the islands of the Indian Ocean. ❋ **OBEN** Bereits im Eingangsbereich macht sich eine Vorliebe für Holz bemerkbar. Auch die Treppe und der Parkettboden betonen diesen Stil. **RECHTE SEITE** Zimmermänner von französischen Schiffen führten auf den Inseln im Indischen Ozean offene Veranden ein. ❋ **CI-DESSUS** Dès l'entrée, prédominance du bois souligné par l'escalier et le parquet. **PAGE DE DROITE** Les charpentiers marins venus de France ont introduit dans les îles de l'océan Indien les varangues, ces vérandas ouvertes.

❋ **ABOVE** The furniture shows how cosmopolitan the island became, with its armchairs and deckchairs from the Compagnie des Indes Orientales. **BELOW** The bedroom with tropical wood panels, softened by immaculately white walls. ❋ **OBEN** Die Möbel, Erinnerungsstücke der Ostindischen Kompanie, zeugen vom kosmopolitischen Geist der Inseln. **UNTEN** Das Schlafzimmer mit einer wertvollen Holzvertäfelung, die durch die strahlend weißen Wände weniger streng wirkt. ❋ **EN HAUT** Les meubles témoignent du cosmopolitisme de l'île avec ces fauteuils et méridiennes, souvenirs de la compagnie des Indes Orientales. **EN BAS** La chambre en boiserie d'essence précieuse adoucie par les murs d'un blanc immaculé.

MAISON FOLIO
La Réunion

Built in the 19th century, the Folio House still has a pristine air,
as though perpetually rejuvenated by the medicinal herbs that grow around it.

The Maison Folio is situated in the heart of the former spa Hell-Bourg at 3,000 feet above sea-level. The village was once a favourite retreat of the island's governor. The prominent colonial families on the island who followed this dignitary's leisurely progress around La Réunion would put in the smaller *cases de changement d'air* (change-of-air houses) that adjoined Maison Folio.

To visit here is to catch a fleeting glimpse of the Ile Bourbon as it once was, given that La Réunion has only just begun to show off its little known colonial heritage, which in the case of some buildings dates right back to the Grand Siècle of Louis XIV. These houses with their painted wood, their colonnades, their steep roofs and latticework tend to have broad *varangues* (verandas) that in some cases run right round the central construction. But to confine our attention to the larger houses would be a pity: the *tit'cases* in the hills also have their points, with their galvanized iron sheets in place of wood and their vivid colours. Here latticework cut from metal sheets perfectly imitates the wooden version in the houses of the affluent. And, just as their owners say, these constructions have nothing to fear, not even cyclones. Before their builders even placed one brick on another, they made sure to secrete in the foundations a mixture of oil, saffron, camphor, shards of copper and a single betel leaf. Thus the stars were sure to be propitiated.

Maison Folio liegt auf 1000 Meter Höhe inmitten des ehemaligen Thermalbades Hell-Bourg. Das Dorf diente früher dem Gouverneur der Insel als Refugium. Die wohlhabenderen kreolischen Familien folgten ihm dorthin und frönten in den kleinen angrenzenden »Hütten« der »Luftveränderung«.

Ein Besuch dieses Hauses beschwört die alte Insel Bourbon herauf, wie Réunion ursprünglich hieß. Die Insel rühmt sich allerdings erst seit kurzem ihres Kolonialerbes. Bis auf einige Besitzungen aus dem 17. Jahrhundert wurden die meisten durchaus beachtlichen Gebäude nicht wahrgenommen. Sie sind aus farbigem Holz, verfügen über Säulengänge, hängende Dächer mit Holzspitzen und eine große offene Veranda, die häufig rund um das ganze Haus verläuft. In dieser Hinsicht sind nicht nur die großen Villen interessant, denn auch die Häuschen in den Hügeln haben viel Charme. Statt wertvoller Hölzer nahm man Blech, die Farben sind greller und die Spitzen aus Metall imitieren die hölzernen der bürgerlichen Villen beinahe perfekt. Außerdem sind die Häuschen sehr solide, nicht einmal Wirbelstürme können ihnen etwas anhaben. Vor den eigentlichen Bauarbeiten wurde eine Mischung aus Wasser, Safran, Kampfer, Kupferstückchen und ein Betelblatt ins Fundament geschüttet, um die Sterne günstig zu stimmen.

La Maison Folio est située au cœur de l'ancienne station thermale de Hell-Bourg. À 1000 mètres d'altitude, le village était le refuge du gouverneur de l'île, suivi dans ses pérégrinations par les grandes familles créoles qui logeaient dans les petites cases attenantes, dites de «changement d'air».

Visiter cette maison, c'est retrouver le visage de l'ancienne île Bourbon. La Réunion commence tout juste à vanter son patrimoine colonial. Méconnu, daté pour certains bâtiments du Grand Siècle de Louis XIV, il est tout bonnement considérable. Construites en bois peint, dotées de colonnades, de toits pentus aux dentelles de bois, ces demeures disposent ici encore d'une grande varangue pouvant tourner autour du corps central de la maison. Mais n'accorder d'importance qu'aux grandes propriétés n'aurait pas de sens. Les «tit'cases» des collines ont elles aussi leur beauté. La tôle remplace le bois précieux, les couleurs explosent. Les dentelles métalliques imitent à la perfection celles des demeures bourgeoises. Et puis, disent leur propriétaire, elles ne craignent rien, pas même les cyclones. Avant de commencer à bâtir, on a pris soin de déposer dans la première fondation un mélange d'eau, de safran, du camphre, des pièces de cuivre et une feuille de bétel. Ainsi, les astres sont amadoués …

❋ **ABOVE AND FACING PAGE** The geometrical motifs and pelmets of the Folio House, enriched by Creole furniture made of wood the colour of the local soil, reflect the refinement of the period. **FOLLOWING PAGES** Whether it takes the form of a large white building with wooden latticework and acid colours, or a small *case* drenched in bright paint, the Creole house has a charm of its own. ❋ **OBEN UND RECHTE SEITE** Die Raffinesse der Kolonialzeit des Maison Folio zeigt sich in den geometrischen Mustern und den kreolischen Möbeln, die aus dem dunklen Holz der Umgebung hergestellt wurden. **FOLGENDE DOPPELSEITE** Die kreolischen Häuser sind einfach zauberhaft: Ob es sich um eine weiße Villa mit bonbonfarbenen Akzenten handelt oder um ein Häuschen aus buntem Blech. ❋ **CI-DESSUS ET PAGE DE DROITE** Les lambrequins et les motifs géométriques de la maison Folio, enrichis de meubles créoles confectionnés dans les bois de couleur du terroir, reflètent le raffinement de l'époque. **DOUBLE PAGE SUIVANTE** Grande case blanche avec ses dentelles de bois et ses couleurs acidulées ou petite case de tôle multicolore, l'habitation créole ne manque pas de charme.

SALIM CURRIMJEE

MAURITIUS

A remarkable house built to the specifications of its architect owner, making extensive use of basic materials and plate glass windows.

Salim Currimjee's seaside holiday home is at the tranquil resort of Poste Lafayette, a place still largely undiscovered by tourists. Its owner simply calls it "the house".

This is a highly complex blend of huge glassed-in spaces with a fine atmosphere of continuity and masses of light. The fundamental, minimalist austerity of all this is a hymn to pure aesthetics and the colours of industrial raw materials. To protect the house from the boom of the sea – and thereby to preserve its intimacy – the façade runs side on to the shore. The use of white and the choice of pale stone for the floors creates a strong connection between interior and exterior, along with constantly shifting light effects in the rooms. The furniture, too, echoes this zen feeling, and the result is that Salim Currimjee's house is unique on the island, a place in which every choice of architecture and decoration has been made in function of the luxuriance of the natural environment and the glory of the view. The bedrooms, which all have terraces of their own, have a muted, turned-inward kind of light, in stark contrast to the reception areas.

Die versteckte Strandvilla liegt in dem beschaulichen Ort Poste Lafayette, der noch weitgehend von Touristen verschont geblieben ist. Der Architekt Salim Currimjee bezeichnet die Villa bescheiden als »Haus«.

Die klaren, großen Räume sind lichtdurchflutet und verstärken durch die Panoramafenster den Eindruck räumlicher Beständigkeit. Die grundsätzliche Schlichtheit, die von der minimalistischen Architektur inspiriert wird, betont die klare Ästhetik und lässt die Farben des Industriematerials hervortreten. Die parallel zum Meer ausgerichtete Fassade hält die Geräusche des Ozeans ab und schützt die Privatsphäre. Die Konzentration auf die Farbe Weiß und die Entscheidung für helle Steinböden sorgen für eine gewisse Kontinuität zwischen dem Äußeren und dem Inneren des Hauses – in den Räumen spielt der beständige Wechsel des Tageslichts eine große Rolle. Die Einrichtung richtet sich nach den Prinzipien der Zen-Philosophie. Die Villa ist auf der Insel einzigartig. Es ist ein Ort, bei dem Architektur und Inneneinrichtung von der Üppigkeit der Natur und der einzigartigen Aussiche bestimmt werden. Die jeweils mit einer Terrasse versehenen Zimmer liegen in gedämpfterem Licht als die Empfangsräume und wirken deshalb wesentlich introvertierter.

Nichée en bord de mer, cette résidence balnéaire est située à Poste Lafayette, un endroit que les touristes n'ont pas encore envahi et où l'architecte Salim Currimjee parle simplement de «maison».

Les vastes espaces dégagés et vitrés, inondés de lumière, renforcent l'impression de continuité spatiale donnée par de grandes ouvertures. La simplicité fondamentale du lieu, inspirée d'une architecture minimaliste, exalte les valeurs de l'esthétique pure et les couleurs des matériaux industriels. Pour protéger la maison de la rumeur de la mer, comme pour préserver son intimité, une façade est orientée parallèlement à l'océan. Le recours au blanc et le choix de la pierre claire des sols génèrent une impression de continuité entre l'intérieur et l'extérieur, un jeu avec des changements permanents de lumière dans les pièces. Le mobilier de celles-ci crée une référence directe à l'ambiance zen. Par son caractère unique dans l'île, cette maison à toutes les qualités d'une résidence de grand standing. C'est un décor où chaque choix a été influencé par l'exubérance de la nature et l'exigence d'une vue superbe. Pourvues de terrasses, les chambres à coucher, baignées d'une lumière plus feutrée affichent un caractère plus introverti, aux antipodes des espaces de réception.

※ **PREVIOUS PAGES** Facing the sea, an architect's dream that is unique on the island. **ABOVE** In the living room, minimalism reigns supreme with simple sofas and a huge bookcase of pale wood. The fundamental simplicity here offsets the nearby presence of the sea. **BELOW** Plate glass windows from floor to ceiling give an effect of airy lightness and transparency. The entire house is a play of black and white. The Dalmatian, also black and white, belongs to the owner.. ※ **VORHERGEHENDE DOPPELSEITE** Beispiellos auf der Insel: ein Architektentraum direkt am Meer. **OBEN** Sofas in strengen Formen sowie eine umfangreiche, in hellem Holz gehaltene Bibliothek bezeugen die minimalistische Haltung auch im Salon. Die natürliche Schlichtheit lässt das Meer noch präsenter erscheinen und verführt zum Träumen. **UNTEN** Die Panoramafenster reichen vom Boden bis zur Decke und verleihen dem Ambiente eine transparente Anmut. Im Inneren des Hauses herrschen die Farben Weiß, Schwarz und Grau vor – wie eine unfreiwillige Anspielung auf das Fell von Salim Currimjees Hund. ※ **DOUBLE PAGE PRÉCÉDENTE** Face à la mer, un rêve d'architecte inédit dans l'île. **CI-DESSUS** Dans le salon, l'esprit minimaliste règne avec des canapés aux lignes sobres et une immense bibliothèque en bois clair. La simplicité fondamentale du lieu renforce la présence de la mer toute proche et incite à la rêverie. **CI-DESSOUS** Les baies vitrées qui vont du sol au plafond assurent un effet de transparence et de légèreté. Dans la maison, il y a partout un jeu de blanc, de noir et de gris, en un écho involontaire au pelage du chien de Salim Currimjee.

❋ **ABOVE** The bedroom has ingenious sliding wooden shutters on its windows to protect it from the sun. **BELOW** The entrance is all cement, glass, white walls and concrete floors. The furniture is resolutely contemporary, and the huge floor-to-ceiling windows give directly on the Indian Ocean. ❋ **OBEN** Ausgeklügelte hölzerne Fensterläden mit Schiebevorrichtung schützen das Schlafzimmer vor der Sonne. **UNTEN** Zement und Glas sind die bevorzugten Baumaterialien im Eingangsbereich. Ergänzt durch weiße Wände und Betonböden entstand ein lichtdurchfluteter, modern möblierter Raum. Die deckenhohen Fenster gehen auf den Indischen Ozean hinaus. ❋ **CI-DESSUS** D'astucieux volets de bois coulissants protègent la chambre du soleil. **CI-DESSOUS** Édifié avec un recours généreux au ciment et au verre, paré de murs blancs, de sols en béton, l'entrée est un espace lumineux aménagé de meubles modernes. Du sol au plafond, les grandes ouvertures donnent sur l'océan Indien.

Mombo Camp ❀

❀ Jao Camp

Botswana

MOMBO CAMP
OKAVANGO DELTA

This camp of huts and walkways built on stilts extends across two kilometres of the African plain.

Living rooms, dining rooms and library form the epicentre of this project by Silvio Rech and Lesley Carstens, in which wood and thatch have been used as basic materials throughout – though none of the trees on the spot were cut down, for obvious reasons.

The rosewood floors are built around the acacias, ebony trees and tall palms which are home to colonies of tiny velvet monkeys. The suites, scattered through the groves of old trees, are lined with khaki canvas stretched between tall wooden pilings pointed skywards. Each tent is divided into two parts; in each one a huge brown and cream-coloured bedroom, with a desk of reddish wood, goes with its own salon area, where there's a broad sofa upholstered in white cotton. In the bathroom, the wood is pale, the light warm and the atmosphere gentle – a real place of relaxation, with tall mirrors, big basins of brown earthenware and a shower right in the middle. Outside, suspended between two palm trees, is another shower directly confronting the savannah. In the distance, vast flocks of birds wheel away into the orange evening sky. The languid outlines of a pride of lions move across the near horizon – another moment of magic in this unspoiled, faraway paradise.

Die Salons, die Speisesäle und die Bibliothek bilden den Mittelpunkt des von Silvio Rech und Lesley Carstens erbauten Gebäudes. Als Baumaterial wurden vor allem Holz und Stroh verwendet – allerdings wurden auf dem Anwesen keine Bäume gefällt, da die Natur als Teil der Einrichtung angesehen wird.

Das Parkett aus Rosenholz windet sich um die Akazien, Ebenholzbäume und hoch gewachsene Palmen, in denen kleine Affen herumturnen. Die um die hundertjährigen Bäume verstreuten Suiten sind mit Khakistoff ausgekleidet, der zwischen hoch ragende Holzpfeiler gespannt ist. Jedes dieser Zelte ist zweigeteilt: Von dem großen Zimmer in Braun- und Cremetönen ist ein kleiner Salon abgeteilt, in dem ein langes, mit weißer Baumwolle bezogenes Sofa steht. Das Badezimmer ist mit hellem Holz ausgestattet und das warme Licht lädt geradezu dazu ein, sich der Faulheit hinzugeben: Hohe Spiegel, weit geschwungene Waschbecken aus braunem Emaille und eine Dusche mitten im Raum schaffen einen Ruheraum par excellence. Eine weitere Dusche hängt zwischen zwei Palmen draußen in der Savanne. In der Ferne schwingen sich Myriaden von Vögeln in den orangefarbenen Himmel. Am Horizont zeichnen sich die Silhouetten friedlicher Löwen ab – so wirkt der Zauber des Augenblicks in diesem vor Menschen geschützten Winkel der Welt.

Les salons, salles à manger et la bibliothèque forment l'épicentre de cet édifice, réalisé par Silvio Rech et Lesley Carstens, où bois et chaume ont été utilisés comme matières premières. Ici, les arbres n'ont pas été abattus, la nature fait partie du décor.

Les parquets de bois de rose tournent autour des acacias, des ébéniers ou des hauts palmiers qu'habitent des familles de petits singes vervets. Les suites, dispersées au milieu des arbres centenaires, sont habillées de toile kaki tendue entre de hauts piliers de bois pointant vers le ciel. Chaque tente est divisée en deux parties. Une immense chambre aux tonalités de brun et de crème, avec bureau en bois cérusé, répond à un coin salon agrémenté d'un large canapé recouvert de coton blanc. Dans la salle de bains, le bois est blond, la lumière chaude, et la paresse douce: une véritable salle de repos avec ses hauts miroirs, ses grandes vasques en faïence brune et sa douche installée au beau milieu de la pièce. À l'extérieur, suspendue entre deux palmiers, on trouve encore une douche face à la savane. Au loin, une myriade d'oiseaux s'envolent dans le ciel orange. Les silhouettes de quelques lions paisibles se dessinent à l'horizon. Magie de l'instant dans ce bout du monde préservé des hommes.

❊ **PREVIOUS PAGE** On the central terrace, the deck chairs offer a stunning vantage point. **FACING PAGE** On the terrace of the "Honeymoon" suite, the *sala*, made up of a daybed in the shade of the palm thatch. Here you can read a book while the big cats snooze nearby. ❊ **VORHERGEHENDE DOPPELSEITE** Von den Korbsofas auf der mittleren Terrasse genießt man den freien Blick auf die Savanne. **RECHTE SEITE** Ein *sala*, ein Ruhebett im Schatten des Palmenblattdaches, auf der Terrasse der »Honeymoon-Suite«. Hier kann man vor einer Kulisse von Großwild lesen. ❊ **DOUBLE PAGE PRÉCÉDENTE** Sur la terrasse centrale, des méridiennes en rotin offrent une vue imprenable sur la savane. **PAGE DE DROITE** Sur la terrasse de la suite «Honey Moon», le *sala*, formé d'un lit de repos à l'ombre d'un toit de feuilles de palme. On lit face aux grands fauves.

※ **ABOVE** In the dining room adjoining the salon, meals are taken at a long *selijna* wood table (*selijna* is a local beech) lit by rows of candles in the evening.
※ **OBEN** Im Speisesaal neben dem Salon werden die Mahlzeiten an einem langen Tisch aus *selijna* (einer hiesigen Buchenart) eingenommen. Abends bei Kerzenlicht wird die Unterhaltung lebhaft. ※ **CI-DESSUS** Dans la salle à manger jouxtant le salon, les repas sont pris sur une longue table en bois de *selijna* (hêtre local). Le soir, les conversations vont bon train à la lueur des bougies.

❋ **ABOVE** In the bedrooms, all of which are built on stilts for maximum security, the tone is minimalist – with African colours, zebra-skin poufs and ostrich-skin lamp shades. **FACING PAGE** A curtain of strung pebbles makes the balcony private. ❋ **OBEN** Aus Sicherheitsgründen wurden die Zimmer als Pfahlbauten errichtet. Sie wurden eher minimalistisch in afrikanischen Tönen dekoriert, mit Zebrafell-gepolsterten Hockern und Lampenschirmen aus Straußenleder. **RECHTE SEITE** Ein Vorhang aus kleinen Steinen schützt den Balkon vor zudringlichen Blicken. ❋ **CI-DESSUS** Dans les chambres montées sur pilotis pour une sécurité maximale, tendance minimaliste aux tonalités africaines avec des poufs en peau de zèbre et des lampes gainées de cuir d'autruche. **PAGE DE DROITE** Un rideau de pierre isole du balcon.

FACING PAGE Each bedroom has its own outside shower under the trees, as an extension of a big bathroom. **BELOW** In the bedrooms, the contemporary furniture designed by Silvio Rech is matched with objects picked up in markets all over Africa. **FOLLOWING PAGES** In the evening, magical dinners are arranged in the *boma* (traditional African stockade). ✳ **LINKE SEITE** Als Verlängerung des großzügigen Badezimmers verfügt jedes Zimmer über eine Freiluftdusche unter den Bäumen. **UNTEN** Die moderne Einrichtung unter Federführung von Silvio Rech wird durch Objekte vom afrikanischen Kontinent aufgelockert. **FOLGENDE DOPPELSEITE** Das Abendessen wird auf märchenhafte Weise in der *boma*, der traditionellen afrikanischen Feuerstelle, zelebriert, die rundherum eingezäunt ist. ✳ **PAGE DE GAUCHE** Chaque chambre dispose d'une douche extérieure placée sous les arbres en prolongement de la vaste salle de bains. **CI-DESSOUS** Dans les chambres, le mobilier aux lignes contemporaines dessiné par Silvio Rech se marie aux objets chinés sur tout le continent africain. **DOUBLE PAGE SUIVANTE** Le soir, des dîners féeriques sont organisés dans le *boma* (cercle traditionnel africain entouré de branches plantées dans le sol).

Jao Camp
Okavango Delta

Guests at this idyllic bush camp come to experience nature at her unspoiled best –
in conditions of high luxury.

It all started with two stubborn people, David and Cathy, authentic pioneers from Maun, the capital of the delta.

Beginning in 1938, David's grandparents too many of Europe's crowned heads on safari, and he himself is a former white hunter. Less is known of Cathy, except that she was always a keen reader of interior decoration magazines. Destiny intervened when, on the off-chance, they entered a competition organized by the government of Botswana. The challenge was to submit ideas for developing a concession in the middle of the delta – and the couple's plan came out top, out of a field of 130. David dreamed of Africa, Cathy of Bali. The South African architects Silvio Rech and Lesley Carstens undertook to bring these two worlds together in terms of architecture and décor, and the result is Jao Camp. Every bedroom opens on a broad terrace with a view of the flaming sunset. Rosewood floors and furniture, muslin mosquito nets, brown earthenware basins were all designed by Silvio Rech and made on the spot by local craftsmen. The huge open salon overlooks the river with its thousands of waterlilies, while among the Zimbabwean jars, *mokuba* cushions and Masai spears, benches and wardrobes imported from Indonesia add a touch of Asia to the décor.

Mit einer gewissen Besessenheit von David und Cathy fing alles an. Die beiden Pioniere stammen aus Maun, der Hauptstadt des Deltas.

Davids Großeltern begleiteten seit 1938 Mitglieder der königlichen Familien Europas auf Safari und er selbst war früher Jäger. Über Cathy ist nicht viel bekannt, außer dass sie aus lauter Langeweile Zeitschriften zum Thema Wohnen und Einrichten verschlang. Ihr Leben veränderte sich schlagartig, nachdem sie sich bei der Regierung von Botswana um eine Konzession mitten im Delta bewarben und unter 130 Bewerbern auserwählt wurden. David hatte nur Afrika im Sinn, sie dagegen Bali. Die südafrikanischen Architekten Silvio Rech und Lesley Carstens konnten dem Paar helfen, diese beiden Welten fruchtbar zu verbinden. Alle Zimmer verfügen über eine große Terrasse mit atemberaubender Aussicht. Nach Entwürfen von Silvio Rech wurde die Einrichtung vom Parkett über die Rosenholzmöbel und Moskitonetze aus Leinenstores bis zu den Waschbecken aus Sandstein an Ort und Stelle von ansässigen Handwerkern hergestellt. Von einem weiträumigen Salon blickt man über den Fluss mit Tausenden von Seerosen. Inmitten der Tonkrüge aus Simbabwe finden sich Kissen aus *mokuba* und Massai-Lanzen. Bänke und Schränke wurden hingegen aus Indonesien importiert, um der Einrichtung ein asiatisches Flair zu verleihen.

À l'origine, il y a l'obstination de David et Cathy, un couple d'authentiques pionniers natifs de Maun, la capitale du delta.

Ses grands-parents à lui, dès 1938, guidaient en safari les familles royales européennes. Il était autrefois chasseur. D'elle, on ne sait pas grand-chose, sinon que pour tromper l'ennui elle dévorait les magazines de décoration. Un coup du sort comme il ne s'en produit qu'un dans une vie a tout fait basculer. Par hasard, juste pour voir, David et Cathy ont proposé au gouvernement du Botswana un dossier d'aménagement d'une concession au cœur du delta. Ils ont été lauréats parmi 130 candidats! Il rêve toujours d'Afrique, elle rêve de Bali. Les architectes sud-africains Silvio Rech et Lesley Carstens ont relevé le défi de réunir les deux mondes. Chaque chambre s'ouvre sur une large terrasse qui offre, le soir, un panorama sur l'horizon flamboyant. Parquet et mobilier en bois de rose, moustiquaire en voile de lin, lavabos en grès aux teintes brunes, l'ensemble, signé Silvio Rech, a été fabriqué sur place par des artisans locaux. Un immense salon ouvert surplombe la rivière et ses milliers de nénuphars. Au milieu des jarres du Zimbabwe, des coussins en *mokuba* et des lances Massaï, les banquettes et les armoires importées d'Indonésie apportent une touche asiatique au décor.

❋ **PREVIOUS PAGES** At the entrance to the camp, which is entirely constructed on tree trunks, is a shop selling African objects. **BELOW** A teak-encircled swimming pool in its own island of greenery near the river, where the hippos sport. **FACING PAGE** When you come in from safari, it's time for a drink by the fire, in the company of an array of percussion instruments (foreground). ❋ **VORHERGEHENDE DOPPELSEITE** Am Eingang des Pfahlbaucamps, im Wirrwarr von Baumstämmen wird in einem Laden afrikanisches Kunsthandwerk verkauft. **UNTEN** Der mit Teakholz eingefasste Swimmingpool liegt im Grünen in der Nähe des Flusses, in dem die Flusspferde schwimmen. **RECHTE SEITE** Wenn man von der Safari zurückkommt, lauscht man bei einem Glas Wein am Feuer den Trommlern (im Vordergrund). ❋ **DOUBLE PAGE PRÉCÉDENTE** L'entrée du camp sur pilotis, avec son capharnaüm de troncs d'arbres, abrite une boutique d'objets africains. **CI-DESSOUS** La piscine cerclée de teck s'inscrit au milieu d'un îlot de verdure à quelques mètres de la rivière où nagent les hippopotames. **PAGE DE DROITE** Au retour du safari, on boit un verre au coin du feu au son d'instruments à percussion (au premier plan).

❋ **BELOW** In the brown salon, the atmosphere is nicely balanced between Asia and Africa. Ghanaian stools and headrests from Zimbabwe stand side by side with graceful Balinese benches and their *kuba* cushions (made of raffia with geometric motifs). **FACING PAGE** Built on stilts for security, the lodge is made up of eight suites distributed among the shady palm trees, each with a glorious view of the river. ❋ **OBEN** Der Salon ist in Brauntönen gehalten, die Atmosphäre hält die Balance zwischen Afrika und Asien. Hölzerne Hocker aus Ghana und Kopfstützen aus Simbabwe harmonieren mit anmutigen balinesischen Sitzbänken und den dazugehörigen Kissen aus *kuba* (geometrisch gemustertem Bast). **RECHTE SEITE** Die aus Sicherheitsgründen als Pfahlbau errichtete Lodge hat acht Suiten, die im Schatten der Palmen verstreut liegen, alle mit unbegrenztem Flussblick. ❋ **CI-DESSOUS** Dans le salon aux tons bruns, l'atmosphère balance entre l'Asie et l'Afrique. Des tabourets du Ghana et repose-tête en bois du Zimbabwe côtoient de gracieux bancs balinais et leurs coussins en *kuba* (raphia aux motifs géométriques). **PAGE DE DROITE** Construit sur pilotis par mesure de sécurité, le lodge est composé de huit suites dispersées à l'ombre des palmiers, avec une vue imprenable sur la rivière.

❋ **ABOVE** The dining room glistens beneath the metal chandeliers designed by Silvio Rech. **FACING PAGE** Just on the edge of the platform, this little store rivals many of the larger rooms in the lodge for beauty and comfort. ❋ **OBEN** Der Speisesaal erstrahlt im Licht der von Silvio Rech entworfenen Metallkronleuchter. **RECHTE SEITE** Der kleine Laden am Rande der Plattform kann es in puncto Schönheit und Komfort mit den schönsten Zimmern der Lodge aufnehmen. ❋ **CI-DESSUS** La salle à manger brille sous des lustres en métal dessinés par Silvio Rech. **PAGE DE DROITE** À l'écart de la plate-forme, cette boutique rivalise en beauté et en confort avec les plus belles pièces du lodge.

❋ **PREVIOUS PAGES** The suites have no partitions, hence the bedroom, sitting room and bathroom form a single space opening on the river. The contemporary-style furniture offsets objects bought all over Africa by the owner. **FACING PAGE** An outside shower. **BELOW** A fine brown earthenware basin designed by Silvio Rech; note the antique bathtub, polished floor and wooden daybed in this bathroom – which is in a corner of the bedroom, there being no partitions. ❋ **VORHERGEHENDE DOPPELSEITE** In den Suiten sind die Zimmer, Salons und Bäder nicht durch Trennwände abgeschlossen, sondern bilden einen großen Raum, der auf den Fluss hinausgeht. Die modernen Möbel passen hervorragend zu den afrikanischen Einrichtungsgegenständen, die die Eigentümerin überall auf dem Kontinent aufgetrieben hat. **LINKE SEITE** Die Freiluftdusche. **UNTEN** Waschbecken aus Sandstein in angenehmem Braunton nach einem Entwurf von Silvio Rech; antike Badewanne, gewachstes Parkett und Ruhebett aus Holz im Badezimmer, das ohne Trennwand in das eigentliche Zimmer übergeht. ❋ **DOUBLE PAGE PRÉCÉDENTE** Les suites ne sont pas dotées de cloisons, ainsi chambre, salon et salle de bains ne forment qu'une pièce ouvrant sur la rivière. Les meubles aux lignes contemporaines se marient parfaitement aux objets chinés sur tout le continent par la propriétaire. **PAGE DE GAUCHE** Douche extérieure. **CI-DESSOUS** Lavabo en grès aux belles teintes brunes dessiné par Silvio Rech; baignoire ancienne, parquet ciré et lit de repos en bois pour cette salle de bains qui ne forme qu'une pièce avec la chambre.

imprint

© 2003 TASCHEN GmbH
Hohenzollernring 53, D-50672 Köln
www.taschen.com

To stay informed about upcoming TASCHEN titles,
please request our magazine at www.taschen.com/magazine
or write to TASCHEN, Hohenzollernring 53, D-50672 Cologne, Germany,
contact@taschen.com, Fax: +49-221-254919.
We will be happy to send you a free copy of our magazine
which is filled with information about all of our books.

Cover:
Design of Dutch Wax Fabric for Vlisco Helmond B.V., Holland, 1992

EDITED BY
Angelika Taschen, Cologne

DESIGN
Sense/Net, Andy Disl and Birgit Reber, Cologne

LITHOGRAPHY MANAGEMENT
Thomas Grell, Cologne

LITHOGRAPHY
lithotronic media gmbh, Frankfurt am Main

PROJECT COORDINATION
Stephanie Bischoff, Christiane Blass, Susanne Klinkhamels, Cologne

TEXT EDITED BY
Christiane Blass, Susanne Klinkhamels, Cologne

ENGLISH TRANSLATION
Anthony Roberts, Lupiac

GERMAN TRANSLATION
Anne Brauner, Cologne

Printed in Spain
ISBN 13: 978-3-8228-4816-6
ISBN 10: 3-8228-4816-6

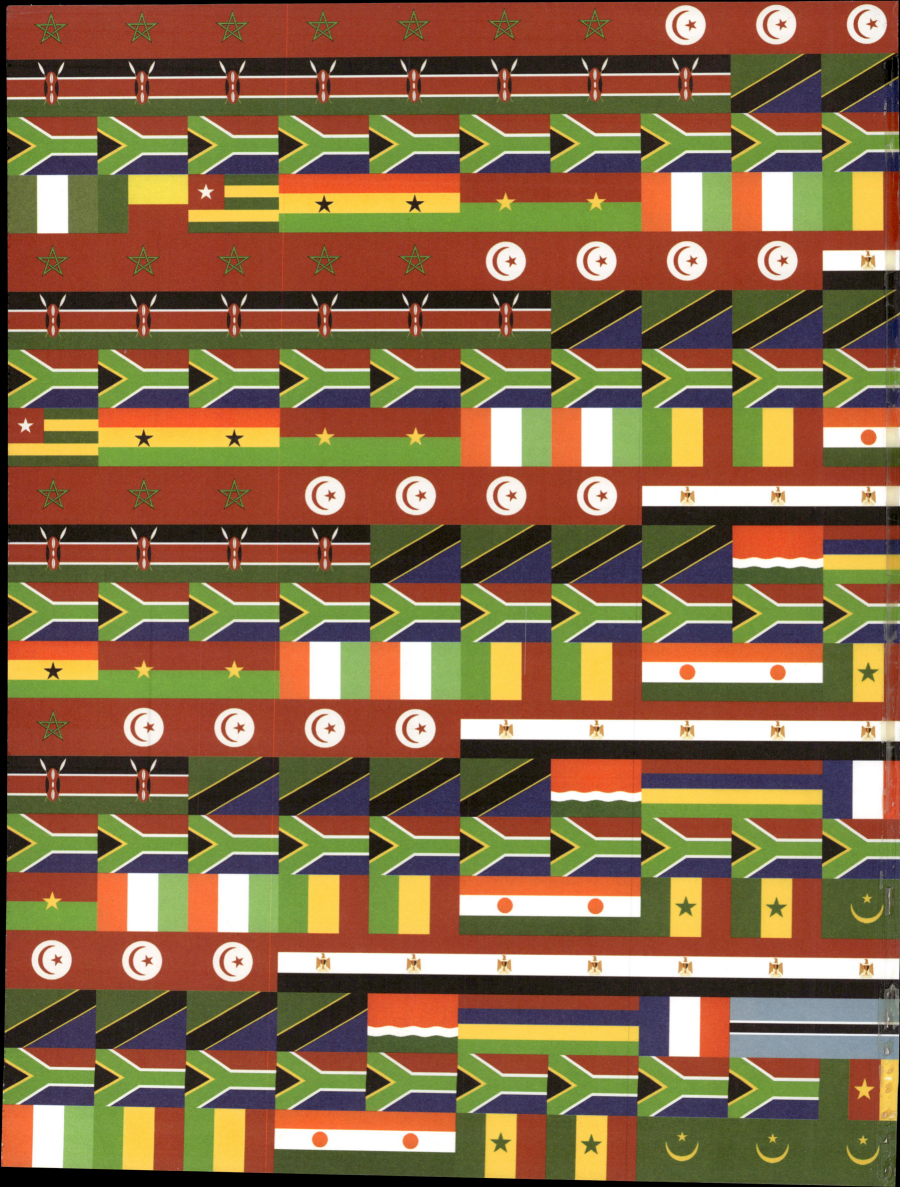

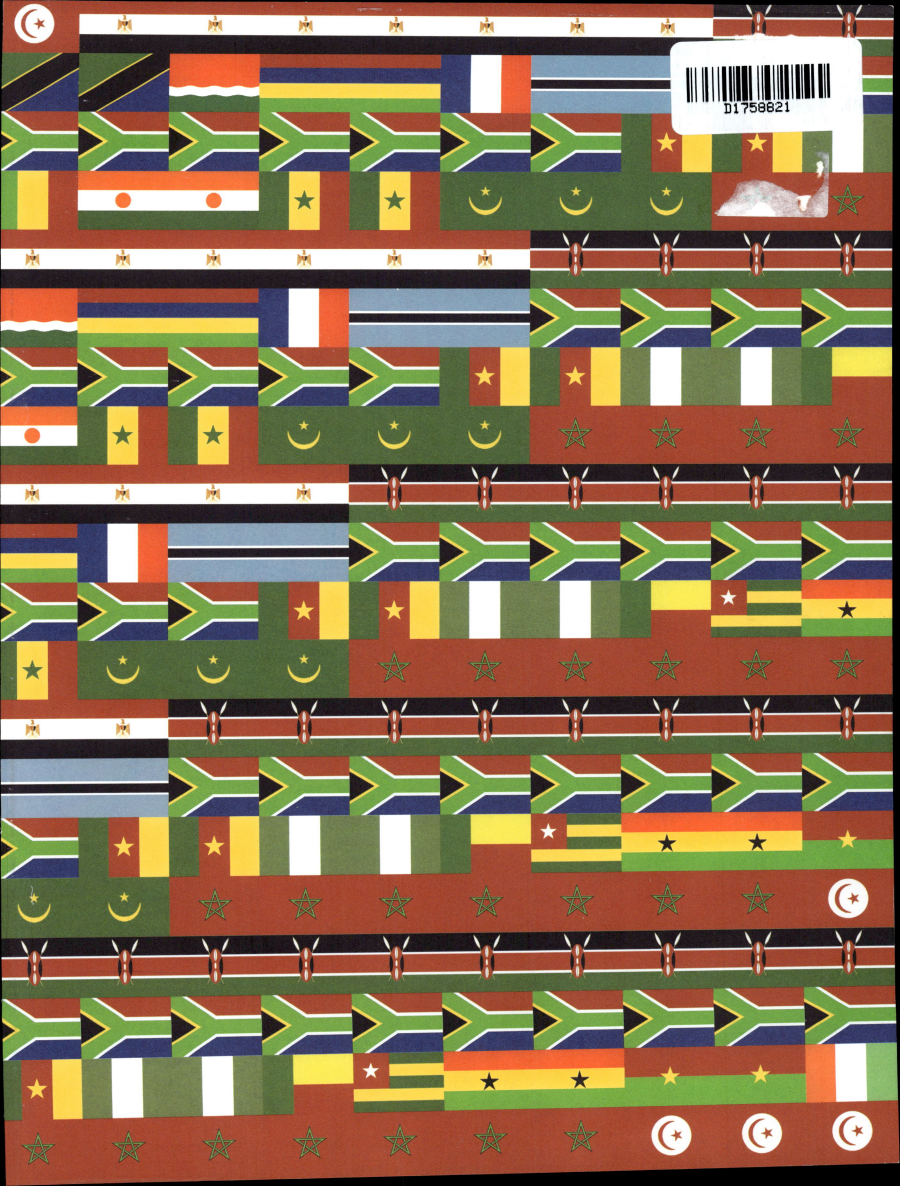